afterlife

Barry Eaton

psychic intuitive

afterlife

Uncovering the Secrets of Life After Death

ALLEN&UNWIN

First published in 2011

Copyright © Barry Eaton 2011

Inspired Living, an imprint of
Allen & Unwin
83 Alexander Street
Crows Nest NSW 2065
Australia
Phone: (61 2) 8425 0100
Fax: (61 2) 9906 2218
Email: info@allenandunwin.com
Web: www.allenandunwin.com

Cataloguing-in-Publication details are available
from the National Library of Australia
www.trove.nla.gov.au

ISBN 978 1 74237 484 0

Set in 12/19 pt Apollo MT by Bookhouse, Sydney
Printed in Australia by Griffin Press

10 9 8 7 6 5 4 3 2 1

The paper in this book is FSC certified. FSC promotes environmentally responsible, socially beneficial and economically viable management of the world's forests.

Dedicated to Anne
*You have always been there to help me heal the
wounds of the past with much patience and love.
Your editing advice is also invaluable.*

Profound thanks also to Maggie Hamilton,
*whose inspiration and confidence in me led to this
book being written.*

In loving memory of Chris Kelly,
*who helped me plumb the depths of my soul to
contact my highest inspiration.*

Contents

Preface

While most people I have spoken with over the years have a belief in some form of life after death, it seems amazing to me that there are so many others who believe absolutely nothing happens after death. They appear happy to accept that after dying the lights simply go out and we completely cease to exist in any way.

The idea that we can be born into such a wonderful world strongly indicates life is not a random event. The clockwork nature of the cosmos does not support the idea of chaos. Life on earth is not some kind of biological accident on a random planet in the solar system. There is a meaning and a purpose to it all.

Finding this meaning is something too few people concern themselves with, unfortunately. It is much easier to let life roll by, than to look at the deeper questions such as who are we, why are we here, where did we come from and where do we go after death?

Death is the great unknown, despite the fact it is our ultimate destination. Perhaps by not thinking about it we hope to somehow put off the inevitable, but there does come a time in life when we are forced to face our mortality.

Where we go after so-called 'death' has always fascinated me. With an inborn acceptance of reincarnation, it has always made sense to me that there has to be something in between our multiple lives. But the big question is: *What*?

When we are born there's no instruction manual, we just have to pick everything up as we go along. The same is true of death. We each have to face it in our own way; we arrive with nothing and leave with nothing.

But is this really the case? Do we arrive with nothing? What about the life energy that fuels our existence, which fades and disappears when the body perishes?

Physics tells us that energy cannot be created or destroyed, that it continues even though it may transform into another form. But where does this energy come from, where does it go and how is it transformed?

To date, scientists have been unable to prove or even explain the existence of a non-physical life. However, I firmly believe that as science and spirituality are slowly drawing closer together in many areas, it will not be long before there are scientific breakthroughs in understanding the afterlife. The Noetic Science movement,[1] an expanded science which acknowledges we are mind, body and spirit, is actively combining objective scientific methods together with humanity's deep inner knowing to explore the whole area of consciousness. Perhaps this is where the breakthrough will be achieved.

Even now, life after death is not a complete mystery. The existence of a world beyond the grave has been embraced by just about every civilisation in recorded history. It is an integral part of many religions and spiritual beliefs and is rooted deep in our subconscious. Intuition and even logic also tell me it is part of our natural soul progression.

The term 'afterlife', which I am using in this book, can be contentious. Ezio De Angelis, one of the best mediums I have ever known, maintains that as there is no such thing as death, then life actually continues in another domain. This means there is not really an *afterlife* as such, but merely another sphere of existence.

For those with an open mind I invite you to join me as I present my research and experiences on the greatest journey of them all. The material in this book comes from my own journey in this lifetime, as well as insights from some of the finest writers and researchers into life after death. As the host and producer of *RadioOutThere.com*[2] I have been privileged to interview these dedicated people over the course of many years.

It may seem a little far-fetched to some that after a long career in broadcasting and journalism I would be interested in the afterlife, let alone want to tap into it. Yet you'd be surprised at the number of people who really want to know more. When it comes down to basics, no matter what we do for a living we are really all souls occupying a body, striving to survive and experience life as we know it on this small planet. The world of spirit for me is like any other mystery. It is just waiting to be explored and the answers are there for all those who seek them.

In the words of J.M. Barrie's immortal character, Peter Pan, 'To die would be an awfully great adventure.'

Let the adventure unfold.

Part A
Dying to go Home

1

A life cut short

A young soldier shivers as the first glimmer of dawn filters across the battlefield. He clutches his rifle closer to his chest and checks the weapon for the umpteenth time to make sure it will not fail him as he anxiously waits for the order to attack.

Despite being early summer there is a chill in the dawn air. Though Brian is only nineteen this is not his first major battle, yet somehow today feels different. Survival is a day-to-day event. Shadowy memories of the many friends and fellow soldiers who have died in the last few months haunt his dreams when he is able to snatch an hour or two of sleep. The unrelenting barrage of artillery and weapons fire are his constant companion.

Brian misses Tosh, a cheerful Cockney who lost his life a few months back. But try as he might the young soldier can't remember which battle took his best mate. They had fought side by side soon after arriving in France and, despite their very different backgrounds, had much in common. Tosh, a veteran at 21, had linked up with the Devons after his own regiment had been all but wiped out and soon took Brian, a fresh-faced soldier, under his wing. They shared many frightening experiences on the front line. Tosh had even got Brian drunk for the first time when they escaped for a few blissful days' leave in a French village.

With an impatient shake of his head Brian brushes aside memories of his friend. There's no room for sentiment in war, and certainly not before a battle. All around him his fellow soldiers are going through their own special rituals as they prepare themselves for yet another onslaught. Their hollow faces reflect their private terror. Each has his own way of getting through the daily horror of trench warfare: some laugh and try to joke; others sit quietly lost in their own world, wondering whether this will be their last day, or whether they can escape by being sent home, seriously wounded and needing hospital care. With a lump in his throat Brian watches a couple of the married men as they exchange letters addressed to loved ones, in case they don't make it. He used to do the same when he first arrived but stopped, worried it might bring bad luck. Most of the men are of similar age to him. All are mud-splattered after the heavy June rain, unshaven and covered in lice. Living on bare rations and tobacco, he sees them growing old and cynical before their time.

As the pale light of sunrise nudges above the horizon they are reminded the attack is imminent. A nervous silence descends until the order is finally passed down the line at 7.30. Bayonets are fixed. Whistles blow. The officers send the regiment scrambling up makeshift ladders and over the top of the trenches. They are to advance at a steady pace, secure the German trenches, then hold their position until further orders.

At first all is quiet as the Devons slowly move down the hillside and into the battle-scarred fields of no man's land. Their artillery has softened up the enemy for the last three or four days, and they dare to hope the Germans have all been killed or have fled their trenches.

But then the bloodshed begins. At first scattered rifle fire comes from the enemy trenches. Then the deadly machine guns follow and a lethal hail of bullets sweeps through the Devons' ranks.

Brian hesitates for a moment, a sudden strange feeling in the pit of his stomach. He knows he's experienced this sensation before, but can't remember when or what it signifies. His sergeant major shouts at him to keep moving.

Brian feels the unexpected impact of the bullets even before he hears the sound of the machine gun aimed in his direction. Without warning there's a ripping, tearing sensation as a bullet thuds into his chest. Then there's two more slamming into his right hip, spinning him around with the force of their impact. Everything seems to be happening in slow motion. As he falls, a mortar shell explodes nearby. The blast hurls him back up and into the air. Then he falls to the ground unconscious.

When Brian regains consciousness everything is silent. For a few moments it's almost as if he's woken from a bad dream, until the painful throbbing in his head reminds him where he is. Trying to raise himself to a sitting position he can't see anything through his left eye. Panic seizes him. Then as the pain sweeps through his body, with a sharp intake of breath he clutches his right side in agony. Trembling violently he forces himself to look down. His hand is sticky with blood. His breath comes in short panting sounds. His head is spinning. Groaning, he sinks back to the ground. There's nothing he can do now except wait for help. Even the slightest movement causes searing pain to rage through his body. Surely someone will come? He tells himself he just has to hang on.

Thirsty. He'd give anything for a drink, but his water bottle is gone. And try as he might he can't find his field dressing to staunch the flow of blood from his right side. Clutching at the deep wound he attempts to raise himself on his left elbow to look for assistance, but it's too agonising. Defeated, he collapses back onto the cold earth. The battle rages somewhere in the distance. As the morning drags on his strength fades.

The loneliness of lying in this godforsaken place so far from home is almost as agonising as the pain. As Brian's eyes close, he sinks into a pit of soft, welcoming darkness. Little did he know then it would be decades before his full story would be understood, or that the reverberation of that battle in France would be felt half a world away.

2

Fear of death

'You don't get to choose how you're going to die. Or when.
You can only decide how you're going to live. Now.'
JOAN BAEZ, SINGER, SONGWRITER AND ACTIVIST

As a young man I was terrified of growing old and dying. There was no special event that I could recall which triggered this fear. I did, however, want to stay young forever.

The only death I had experienced was my grandfather, who passed away peacefully in his bed. My parents protected us from the upset, so I don't remember even attending my grandfather's funeral, or any other funeral for that matter. There were no nightmares to create this very real fear I had. Even so, I can still now remember this strong fear of death during my teenage years. As time passed this fear faded, only for it to resurface as I began writing this book.

So what of my fear of death? A wise man who helps people to prepare for death once told me that those who fear death have put nothing back into life. Looking back, I guess this applied to me as a teenager, as at that stage I had certainly only been a taker. The time of giving back was yet to come.

We all have major turning points in our lives, which often come in accepting the death of the old so we can birth the new. One such occasion emerged after my second divorce, just as I was putting my life together again, or so I thought.

It began with a blind date. The person I took out introduced me to her friend Judy. No immediate bells rang when we first met, but a few days later at a group dinner our eyes met and, as she later told me, Judy thought, 'I am going to spend the rest of my life with this man.'

Her intuition was working well that night.

Events moved pretty swiftly. We ended up travelling around Europe together a few weeks later. By this stage we realised that there was a huge connection between us and when we returned home we started living together.

Life with Judy was never easy or predictable, but it was a fabulous experience. We shared many loves and interests from spiritual matters to rugby. Judy reignited my love of family which had all but disappeared during my last marriage. We shared many hours of spirited discussion and soon found we shared similar beliefs. By this stage I was working as an astrologer and clairvoyant, on top of my radio broadcasting work. Judy would accompany me to psychic events and round up potential clients for readings. We were a very successful team.

One of our favourite escapes was a couple of hours out of the city, where we stayed in an historic former 'pump house' which belonged to Judy's friend Diane, as we loved the mountain scenery. There were many discussions about eventually moving to the mountains. We even had a block of land picked out.

A year before Judy and I met I had connected with a spirit guide, TM, who encouraged me to open my mind to do automatic writing so he could pass on detailed messages. Automatic writing is triggered by completely clearing the mind and allowing the pen to start writing. It is not even necessary to look at the paper while writing as the pen soon has a mind of its own. Afterwards it is often surprising to see what has been written.

Automatic writing was easier than I first thought and the messages soon started flowing, offering positive guidance. One message stood out. I would meet a special woman the following year. Our time together would be short but we would achieve a lot together.

Judy and I both intuitively knew we had shared many past lives together. Intrigued, we went to see a past-life specialist who told us we had suffered many short relation-ships, most ending in tragedy. It seemed we were the original star-crossed lovers. I was regressed to a life in the 19th century when I was a casualty of the American Civil War. I watched as my wife in that lifetime, now Judy, wept as she cradled my dead body in her arms. I have always had a fascination with the Civil War so this revelation came as no surprise on many levels.

Unfortunately this lifetime was to continue the pattern of the past, as is often the case. Judy and I had only been together for a little less than four years when she collapsed one night with a heart and lung condition and was rushed to hospital. She had been suffering ill health for a few months prior to her collapse, but we both believed she was able to be healed. Two months later she passed away.

I was devastated. It had taken more than 50 years for me to meet my soul mate, only to have her snatched from me. The four years we spent together, however, were wonderful and intense, and we shared experiences that would take most couples three times as long to achieve.

My earlier fear of death now turned into a desperate need to be with Judy. If I could have walked through a door and joined her I would gladly have done so, but it wasn't to be. Little did I realise that Judy's death was to be the re-awakening of my connection with the world of spirit.

My spiritual awakening had already received a boost with the breakdown of my second marriage. Studies in astrology followed, as I looked for answers to life's mysteries.

Suddenly there were more questions than answers. Astrology taught me a lot about self-knowledge and acceptance, and it also triggered my intuition. Seven years later Judy's death opened the portals of the spirit world to me. Like so many who grieve, I had a real reason to explore the afterlife in depth.

Losing someone you love is heartbreaking. But more often than not there is a gift for the surviving partner when people pass away. Sometimes it is hard to see what this gift is, as emotions tend to cloud our mind. My gift was the opportunity to communicate with those in the world of spirit. As this gift developed it began to accelerate my interest and growth in spiritual matters. Gradually my work as a broadcaster took second place, because this new world was so fascinating.

At the time of Judy's passing we were running a radio program called *Celestial Power*. No prizes for guessing the theme! The title was given to us one night by Judy's deceased father, Bill. This was quite fitting as Bill had been an off-course bookmaker in his previous life and he gave us a great racing tip, a horse named Celestial Power. It romped in the following Saturday at 14 to 1, so of course we just had to use the name for the show. *Celestial Power* was the start of a successful program that evolved into my current program *RadioOutThere.com*. Unfortunately there were no more racing tips from Bill after that. He was obviously a one-tip pony!

A few months after Judy passed over I was anxious for news from her in spirit, even if it was only to confirm my belief in the afterlife. Quite often a medium's messages from loved ones on the other side are simply 'survival evidence', letting you know they still exist. Survival evidence comes in many forms. It may be a message about the way they died or some other personal detail unknown to the medium. Spirit is very clever at choosing details only a loved one would know about. This can be enough for those left behind who are grieving, desperately wanting something to hold on to.

One of my most popular guests on *Celestial Power* was Ruth Wilson, a well-known and talented medium. Ruth met Judy only a week or so before her passing, but three months later Ruth rang me unexpectedly. Judy had come to her from spirit and wanted to contact me. This filled me with delight.

The morning of the appointment I turned up half an hour late, as I was still full of grief and very confused, and had written the wrong time in my diary. Ruth was waiting for me impatiently at her front door and whisked me into her living room, saying, 'Judy has a whole lot of people waiting for you. You're late.' I looked around the room and thought they must be hiding in cupboards or something, because I couldn't see a soul anywhere. It turned out the room was actually full of *souls*. My parents, an uncle or two, a cousin not long passed over, and a lot of other deceased family members and friends were there. Judy had organised the gathering as my advance Christmas present. She described each of them to Ruth, who then passed on appropriate messages to me.

Ruth was stunned at the turnout, as she did not know anything about my family and had only met Judy fleetingly. 'Does she normally do things like this?' Ruth asked. I burst out laughing, because gathering this amount of people together was Judy's cheeky dig at me for what had happened on the last Christmas Day we shared before she died.

She had invited a house full of people for what was to be her last Christmas dinner on earth. There was so little room left that I ate my festive meal at a kitchen benchtop, standing up and grumbling loudly the entire time. If ever I needed proof of survival evidence, that gathering in Ruth's living room was enough for me!

Ruth also told me about Judy's reactions to a couple of other very personal events that were playing out in my life at that time, things which Ruth could not have known. This gave me further proof of contact. Later Ruth told me that I had been 'given permission' to contact Judy directly and instructed me how to do it.

Spirit is wonderful in the way it prepares us for what we most need, often months, if not years, ahead. By this stage I was already versed in automatic writing and psychic communication, following on from my studies in astrology, so this was how Judy and I started our communication.

Ruth told me that I was to find a little bell and ring it as the signal to make contact with Judy. She explained that spirit communication is generally through thought and images, but that at first I would be able to use my automatic writing to get used to the idea of talking with those in spirit. I found it all rather easy. Maybe somebody was prodding me from the other side. When I wanted to contact Judy all I had to do was find a private place, clear my mind, ring the bell and wait patiently for her, pen in hand. I knew when she was with me as her voice came through very clearly into my mind.

Those first few sessions were very emotional as we exchanged personal messages. They were often short and sweet; no deep and meaningful information. There was, however, a problem over the terms of Judy's will which involved me. Her advice from spirit helped me to find a resolution and avoid conflict.

As I developed my medium skills over the next couple of years the automatic writing gave way to direct channelling, something I had always been very sceptical about up to that time. I discovered mediumship was about being able to tune my energy into the thoughts, images and voices coming from the spirit world, like tuning in a radio or TV station. The messages were all around me once I opened my mind and heart. It was simply a matter of finding the right frequency and trusting what was being transmitted. Trust is the vital ingredient. This is only achieved after much trial and error. I soon realised mediumship is a natural extension of clairvoyance.

When starting a session I had to do a meditation and clear my mind of any anxiety or concerns, and present my mind as an empty vessel to establish and maintain contact. I found it very comforting to know that Judy and I were still able to communicate and I had not lost her as I had feared. It was also good to know that Judy could communicate with me after such a short time in the afterlife. I discovered it takes a lot of energy for those in spirit to be able to speak with us and that a lot of work goes into making contact from their side.

Judy stayed with me for several years as I hosted my radio programs and conducted spiritual groups and intuitive counselling sessions. She would bring people through from spirit. I dubbed her my 'spirit wrangler' as she deftly organised people at the other end of the line—just as she had done at all those psychic events. She also came through to me personally, firstly with words of comfort, and then with messages of advice and inspiration.

She has now moved on in her spiritual evolution and our contact these days is very rare. However, some of our experiences and her revelations are contained in these pages. My own adventures since then have taken me in many different directions, including working with mediums from all over the world. These and other experiences have convinced me there is no such thing as 'death'. Life is merely an ongoing spiritual adventure. As we move from experience to experience we have the chance to evolve as a soul.

It's not all serious stuff. Frequently there's room for a laugh. When one of the members at my tennis club called out loudly one day, 'Hey, Barry, I believe you talk to dead people', I was able to truthfully say 'No'. If he had pursued the matter, I could have told him I only converse with live people who have passed on from this plane of existence.

The journey in between lives is a vital aspect of our soul's growth. Every person's story is different, just as it is on earth, but there are common factors that apply to us all.

My inter-life journey and research began when I was taken into deep trance and 'opened up to spirit' by Chris Kelly, an amazing healer, trance medium and shaman. While in this state I was connected with my guide, M. The ability to travel back through time during meditation was also given to me at this time.

So with M guiding my footsteps, my visionary meditations and my fingers on the keyboard, I'd like to share my fascinating exploration of the great beyond.

3

The next world

My first contact with Judy, made possible by Ruth, inspired me to learn as much as I could about the afterlife. I wanted to know where it was located, what it was like there, what Judy was doing. My enquiring mind knew no bounds.

One of the wonderful things about setting off on this kind of journey is the magical way synchronicity comes into play. Books started appearing, either through recommendation, or sometimes literally falling off the shelf as I was browsing in a bookshop. Without even asking for it out loud, my education had begun. As Judy and I conversed I was also able to get her side of the picture. My radio program also proved invaluable with some wonderful guests often popping up with perfect timing to answer the questions I had.

I'm sure I'm not alone with my questions. One of the greatest mysteries of life is what happens when we die.

For many of us our fear of death prevents us from actively pursuing our real purpose. When we remove as much of the mystery around death as possible, life opens up in many ways.

The best way to start our afterlife journey is simply to accept that when our body passes its use-by date you do not really die or disappear forever. Instead, you simply pass from one state of reality to another. While we're on earth, in essence we are a spiritual being in a human body. Death is the severing of this relationship, which means our spirit can return to its origins. As M explained, that's what happened to me in my last life when I was that young soldier Brian, who died during the Battle of the Somme in 1916, but more on that later. The important thing to realise is that we are all immortal.

So, what about this life and the one before?

Our physical body, though we often forget it, is simply a vehicle that allows us to experience our journey through earthly life. Surrounding us is our aura, which is made up of several layers. The first layer, closest to our physical body, is the etheric body, essentially our life energy. It runs through all the major organs, glands, nerves and energy centres supporting and sustaining our physical body. It impacts our health and life energy. The etheric body is invisible to most people. It is what we see when we begin to view auras, and looks the same as the physical body. This first layer fades and disappears a few days after death.

The next layer, the astral body, is best described as our mind, or consciousness. After the energy from the etheric body is cut off after death, the astral body returns to what are generally known as the astral planes. Here, there are many different levels or planes of existence. Our soul is guided to its appropriate level, according to our development. Our astral body knows the astral world well, as it is accustomed to travelling there all through our life, usually when we are asleep. The astral body is attached to our physical body by a very fine silver cord. This cord allows us to return to our body after astral travelling at night. Once the cord is cut, in what we refer to as death, our physical body perishes and our astral and physical bodies separate permanently.

After the physical body perishes, the life force is trans-ferred to the etheric body for a short period of time. This helps us to adjust to the new conditions. After that the life force passes on to our astral body for the next stage of its journey back to the spiritual realm. This process is a bit like catching different forms of transport to get to our ultimate destination.

The earth plane is far denser than the astral plane and the higher spiritual realms beyond that. These planes also vibrate at much faster rates, which is why they are invisible to us. Over a period of what we understand as 'time', we acclimatise to our new state of being.

Our spirit is a form of energy that powers our body during earthly life. When it departs the body dies. You only have to see a dead body to realise the life force has departed. The spirit, however, being pure energy, lives on. Believe it or not, the soul can even be weighed. In one bizarre recorded experiment, a man was weighed by his doctor just before and immediately after death. The difference was found to be approximately ¾ ounce (21 grams).

Our higher self (Ego) is pure spirit. It's that part of us which is immortal. The higher self resides in the world of spirit and controls the other three bodies: the physical, etheric and astral. This is different to the small ego, which is essentially our personality, and which drops away once we pass on. So, when we talk about being immortal, or of being pure spirit, we're actually talking about our divine or higher self.

Once we learn how to communicate with our higher self through meditation, we gain access to an inner storehouse of wisdom and guidance. Our spirit guides utilise this energy source to inspire and advise us.

We need never feel alone again.

4

The soul's path

'Death—the last sleep? No, it is the final awakening.'
Sir Walter Scott, author and poet, 1771–1832

The more I delved into this area, the more I came to realise the way the soul separates from the body varies with each person. When Judy spoke to me for the first time through Ruth, she recalled that when her time came to leave this life, a pair of soft hands were extended to her. 'I was gently lifted clear of my physical body,' she explained.

Judy was fortunate as she had prepared for her 'curtain call'. This may seem a strange thing to say, but it is something that many people with a spiritual or religious background do, as it makes the transition much easier. Judy was counselled by Peter Ramster in her final weeks and he helped her heal spiritually before she passed over. This meant she was able to tie up a lot of loose ends from this lifetime. Peter is a talented psychologist, skilled in dream therapy, as well as in past-life regression. He later told me that during the night before Judy's passing, he had a dream of two white doves landing on the windowsill next to her hospital bed and calling her soul to leave the body. Her soul then took on the appearance of a third dove, after which they all flew away together. The image stayed with us both for many weeks. Some time later I realised that Peter had not been to the hospital where Judy was admitted the night before her passing, so he had no idea of the layout of the ward. Judy was in a large room and had the only bed adjacent to the window. Peter's dream took on new significance for us both after that.

Many people believe that angels take on the form of birds when they come to earth. Perhaps that is where the image of angel's wings was born. Several months before her death Judy told me about a dream in which she was visited by an angelic presence, who gave her the choice of staying in a pain-wracked body or returning to spirit. At the time I selfishly prayed she would stay, but I now know she made the right choice.

So, where do we go when we return to spirit?

There are several directions the soul, now an astral body, can go after 'death'. Most souls are guided gently by loved ones who have already passed over and are waiting to escort them on their journey back to the spirit realms. But others can refuse to move on from the earth plane.

They are held here by such things as physical cravings, for example drugs or sex. They can also remain because of a fear of the unknown. This fear of moving on is often related to the way the person has conducted themselves in life, perhaps believing they will be cast into some flaming hell to pay for their sins. Some can't accept they have died, or are very attached to a place or person, so they wander around lost and aimless, sometimes for centuries of earth time. This is what happens with ghosts and haunted places.

There are also those who find themselves in a dark and eerie world, in the lower astral plane of existence, closest to the earth. Souls are often at that level because of their own beliefs that there is nothing after death or as a result of their less-than-ideal activities in the life just ended. This plane of existence has been given many names. Many refer to it as purgatory. It is a part of the 'Bardo' in Buddhism, the Umbral region to Spiritists, and the Gehinnom in Judaism. The great psychic Edgar Cayce described it as the 'Plane of Darkness', where the soul is cut off from love and hope while it goes through a period of deep reflection. Whatever label we use, it is essentially a kind of halfway house between the earth plane and the spirit world. The soul experiences a sense of lovelessness and hopelessness because at that stage they feel beyond love and hope.

The soul that finds itself in the lower astral plane goes through a time of intense reflection and cleansing before being admitted into the higher realms of the spirit world. There are several different levels on the lower astral plane. This is most likely where the concept of 'hell' emerged. The good news is that there is actually no such thing as hell. The only 'demons' you come across are those created by your own mental state—though they can appear very real. Helpers and guides from the higher realms visit the lower astral constantly to assist in healing individual souls. No one has to remain in darkness forever, as we are part of a loving universe. To put it in another way, no one is beyond love and hope.

American channel Carolyn Evers has a fascinating account of how she contacted the spirit of Julius Caesar in the lower astral.[1] He had been stuck there since his death in 44 BCE. Caesar talked of his guilt when he looked back on a lifetime of killing, maiming, enslaving, looting and creating misery for hundreds of thousands of people. He told Evers there is no such thing as death. After his assassination he lived for many years surrounded by what he described as a grey world, where he was in a constant state of agony and mental numbness. As much as he wanted to, he was prevented from progressing to the next level, even though he knew of its existence.

This stasis only served to intensify his anguish. He described the next step, which was denied to him, as a state of happiness and beauty. Whenever a portal of light opened for someone else to progress to this next level he rushed to it, but each time was refused entry. The frustration he experienced at this loss of his power demonstrated graphically to him what he had done to others during his life, by selling countless people into hopelessness and slavery. His triumph as one of history's greatest generals meant nothing in this drab grey domain, as he was forced to relive again and again his cruel and heartless actions. He felt not only powerless, but also suffered the ignominy of a life that had brought so much pain and sorrow to so many. Caesar finally came to realise that nobody was punishing him for his actions. It was his own mind that was his tormentor.

Caesar talked of many of his generals, legionnaires and followers, who chose to stay loyal to him and therefore suffered the same consequences for their greed and cruelty, constantly reliving their past deeds in the same grey mist. However, Caesar said all was not hopeless, as advanced souls came down from the higher levels to help with their education and healing. Evers revealed that the spirit of Caesar's daughter, Julia, was eventually able to help her father move on from his brutal past-life deeds and gain entry to the next level.

The concept of 'old souls' is worth exploring. There is a tendency to think that old souls are all wise. My guide M confirmed that describing someone as an old soul is not necessarily a compliment. We only return to the earth plane to learn and evolve, so the older the soul the more they have had to return as the lessons are not being learned. Although there are also highly advanced souls that agree to return to help in troubled times or periods of world transformation, generally speaking the older the soul, the slower the soul growth. Now that's food for thought!

Some souls seem to get 'lost' for a while or do not wish to move on, but a soul is never really lost. The decision not to cross over is an individual one. Members of spiritualist churches regularly have group sessions to help those stuck on the earth plane, or elsewhere, to cross over into the light. The more we learn about these dynamics, the more we realise how much our earthly life, and our head space, matters.

5

Clearing a haunted house

When a soul refuses to cross over to the spirit world after death, it can linger around the earth plane for a long time. Fear of the unknown, or a refusal to accept they are dead, are just two of the many reasons they do not move on. These spirits remain stuck in a world where they are unseen and ignored by the people around them.

Kate Barnes, a medium and clairvoyant, and regular guest on my radio program, rang me out of the blue one day to ask if I would work with her 'clearing' a house. It was located on a main street in an old inner city suburb. For many years this area was the haunt of criminals, drunks and the homeless, before it became fashionable in the 1980s. The occupants had been driven out of the house earlier that day after a series of strange and unnerving incidents and would not return until the 'ghosts' had been moved on.

Experiencing a series of loud noises and bumps was one thing, but when the woman of the house felt a hand on her back trying to push her down the stairs that morning, they fled. Kate was a bit daunted by the situation and naturally wanted a little support.

As Kate and I were walking along the street towards the house, I had a sudden vision of a trapdoor being opened and light flooding into a dark cellar. When we arrived at the three-storey terrace house, it was still unlocked after the residents' hasty departure that morning. When we walked inside we immediately encountered a heavy atmosphere. Climbing the stairs we started to feel the presence of not one but several spirit energies.

Kate is a visual medium. At the time I mainly received messages either through clairaudience (hearing messages) or by thought communication (telepathy). Between us, we first connected with an old sailor who had died many years previously and didn't want to move on from his familiar surroundings. We managed to convince him that he was 'dead' and, after a lot of persuasion, his mother's spirit came to collect him and take him into the light.

Realising there was another very strong energy in the front bedroom, we connected with a male spirit, who told us he had been killed in a motorbike accident nearby several years earlier. He had been a rough and tough bikie in his life, and realising he had died in the accident he went straight into this house to hide and avoid being 'sent to hell'. When the residents of the house began renovating, he got upset and tried to get rid of them by scaring them away in his old crude manner.

It took some time but we finally persuaded the spirit there was no such thing as hell, and that he wasn't going to be punished for being a bikie. We then managed to help him move into the light, to cross over. Interestingly, when I related this to a journalist friend a few weeks later, he remembered the story of a well-known local bikie leader who had been killed in an accident almost outside that very same house.

Kate and I figured by then that we must have sorted the problem, and we told the residents of the house what had transpired, assuring them it was safe to return home. But something was still niggling my mind. Just as we were leaving, I mentioned my vision of the trapdoor and the man's mouth dropped open in amazement. He pulled back a large rug that covered the living room floor, to reveal a trapdoor. We opened it and discovered an old cellar. With some trepidation we went down to explore the inky depths, and as I looked up at the floor above us the sunlight streamed down to my feet exactly as it had appeared in my vision.

The floor of the cellar was bare, hard-packed earth. Both Kate and I had a feeling that if we cared to bring down picks and shovels we would most likely find something bony. The cellar had apparently been sealed over for many years, so, after some quiet deliberation, we decided whoever or whatever was under the ground needed to stay there. We shut the trapdoor and walked away. I felt a strong sense of relief, and to this day I feel that a spirit somewhere is now able to rest in peace.

My experience in this inner city house also taught me a valuable lesson—spirit helpers are always available to assist these disoriented souls, often with the assistance of mediums.

6

Where do we go after death?

'Life is pleasant. Death is peaceful.
It's the transition that's troublesome.'

ISAAC ASIMOV, AUTHOR, 1920–92

Until I started learning about the realms of the afterlife, like many people I was led to believe there were two places we could end up after death—heaven or hell. If we went to heaven we winged our way up to the pearly gates where St Peter was waiting to let us in. Otherwise we descended into the fiery pits of hell to be tormented for all time. Not much of a choice really. Thankfully we're moving beyond this narrow view as we learn more about the afterlife.

All spiritual beliefs say that everyone goes somewhere after what we call death—but where?

Seth, a spirit channelled by medium and author Jane Roberts in a series of 42 books, says that the afterlife does not exist in just one place, so it has no specific location.[1] These 'environments', as he refers to them, do exist but we cannot perceive them because of our physical limitations. This suggests that the spirit world is all around us, perhaps in a different dimension of reality. It certainly helps explain the 'tunnel experience' of leaving the body, which happens to many people who have out-of-body experiences. It's almost as if the tunnel is a kind of wormhole linking these dimensions.

Writer, researcher and former engineer Bruce Moen has made countless journeys into the unknown. He describes the afterlife as part of the non-physical world, a vast space which contains many different places or levels of existence. Where we eventually 'land' in the afterlife is mostly determined by the beliefs and expectations we have created during our life in the physical world. For example, fanatically religious people who believe that only the followers of 'their faith' go to heaven, find themselves surrounded by their own kind. They continue their very restricted lives until they eventually begin to question and explore the real nature of the afterworld.

Moen suggests people who believe there is nothing after death find themselves in a black void, until eventually they realise that this in itself is a kind of existence. When their belief system expands, they're finally able to progress to other levels. He describes the location of the afterlife as surrounding the earth, expanding outwards in an unending movement.

British physicist Sir Oliver Lodge, who was involved in the development of the wireless telegraph, believed that there was *something* between our planet and the sun. He described it as millions of times denser than water, otherwise, he said, there would be nothing to stop earth from crashing into the sun.

But the question remains: Where are these other planes of existence actually located? Some religions speak of heaven and hell being located in opposite directions. You go up to heaven if you're good and down to hell if you're bad. That concept was designed for lawless societies of the past that needed simple answers. Today we're a much better educated society, and find that concept increasingly hard to embrace.

7

The vastness of the spirit world

Just as there are many countries on earth there are many planes of existence in the spirit world. The majority of us go to what Frederic Myers calls the 'Plane of Illusion'. He locates this on the third plane and believes it is the light at the end of the tunnel many people describe that links earth with the afterlife.

Myers was a Professor of Classics at Cambridge University in England more than a century ago. Fascinated with the afterlife, he founded the first Society for Psychical Research in 1882. Myers grappled with the question of contact from beyond the grave, and when he died in 1901 his work continued with communications from the spirit world.

To avoid scepticism he sent his messages through a variety of people in England, America and India. The messages on their own did not make sense, but when joined together in jigsaw fashion, they formed a cohesive picture.

These communications continued for some 30 years as Myers proved his messages were not created in the mind of one medium. Quite often the person receiving their message had no idea what it meant. From 1901 to 1932 more than 3000 scripts were communicated.

Like all those in spirit, Myers had great difficulty in sending messages from the other side. 'I appear to be standing behind a sheet of frosted glass which blurs sight and deadens sound, dictating to a reluctant and somewhat obtuse secretary,' he explained. Despite these difficulties, Myers sent through an enormous amount of details of life in the spirit world, all received by automatic writing.

According to Myers the 'Plane of Illusion' is very similar to life on earth. He described beautiful, peaceful surroundings where people live in communities in earth type houses. They eat, drink, play sport and even go to work. Life seems to continue from where it left off on earth, but without the stress. Every pleasure the heart desires or the mind creates is available here, and manifested by the individual's thoughts, either consciously or unconsciously. So, if someone wants a lovely house to live in, full of beautiful furniture, they can create it simply by visualising what they desire. Myers explained this lifestyle is readily adopted by those spirits who previously believed this type of existence is what heaven is all about. Such a place explains the large variety of descriptions we get via mediums about life in the great beyond.

This sounds ideal—a real paradise—but after a while it begins to pall and boredom sets in, as everything comes too easily, without challenge. Myers says that when the soul is ready it is then assisted to either find ways of accessing higher planes or return to earth for another life.

During our time on the Plane of Illusion we still have access to our families and friends on earth and, at the same time, are in constant contact with our spiritual guides, as our learning and spiritual growth continues. So it would seem there are still certain responsibilities, even in paradise.

The next level, the fourth plane, Myers calls the 'World of Idealised Form', where all desire to have any earthly contact disappears as the soul explores avenues beyond the confines of the earth plane. Reincarnation is now unnecessary in this beautiful world 'free of rigid intellectual structures and dogmas'. The mind, given new freedom, starts to learn how to create an infinite variety of forms, to access energies and colours way beyond our imagination. Only evolved souls are able to access this and further higher planes. Essentially, Myers says, we have to earn our place to be admitted.

The fifth level he calls the 'Plane of Flame'. Here spirits take on a body of flame, so they can explore the universe for cosmic understanding without being harmed by temperatures or turbulence. The exploring soul is able to return after each journey with a fuller understanding of these cosmic reaches. On this plane we are no longer in a form as we understand it; instead, we become what is best described as an 'outline'. Each soul is now part of a group soul, while still retaining aspects of their individuality as they advance.

The sixth level is the 'Plane of Light' where the inhabitants are evolved souls. By this stage these souls have lived through all aspects of the created universe and they have completed their growth. They have left behind all need for matter and form and exist purely as white light. Here, pure reason reigns supreme. Emotion and passion, as we understand it, are absent. These souls are now white light, and according to Myers 'the pure thought of their Creator'.

The seventh 'Plane of the Spirit Realm' is the domain of God or the Creator. Myers, who was not a religious man, describes this final plane of being as dwelling not only out of time, but outside of any universe. He describes it as 'the passage from form into formlessness. It is an existence that has no need to express itself in a shape, however tenuous, however fine. The soul who enters into the seventh state passes into the beyond and becomes one with God.'

My guide M confirmed that the vast majority of souls from earth are living in the third plane. However, there are several different sub-spheres to this plane, where the soul can learn and progress before finally reaching the fourth level, the world of idealised form. This only happens after many incarnations.

Prior to my research into the life and work of Frederic Myers, I had been able to connect and converse with beings on the fourth plane through meditation. This happened after I purchased two amazing crystals while seeking healing at John of God's Casa de Dom Inácio in Brazil.[1] I was then told by the doctors in spirit to meditate, raise my vibration level and open my heart to the spirit world.

Journeying firstly to the fourth plane I was in awe of the colours and the beauty surrounding me. There was the deepest feeling of peace at this level, which embraced me in a very loving and gentle way. The freedom from restrictions of the past, which is found on this plane, was explained to me. Now I finally understood how our earthly emotions and beliefs restrain and separate us from the higher realms. Given the choice I would have stayed here, but I was told that this plane is where I must aspire to for the next stage of my soul's growth.

After an amazing series of meditations, reaching what I later discovered was the fifth plane, the 'Plane of Flames', I was subsequently instructed by M to 'raise your vibrations to the sixth dimension'. After realising this intention I felt an amazing sensation of my spirit rising out of my body. I had no idea of what the sixth dimension represented at this stage, but as my vibrations raised I felt a wonderful sense of love and peace embrace me, even more intense than that of the fourth plane.

In one of these meditations I was shown—in the form of a pure white light—an image of the beings that were helping me. I was then told this was how life expressed itself in the sixth level, and was also able to tune into a very powerful healing energy. These beings told me to use this energy in turn to help others in their healing.

Imagine my surprise and delight several weeks after making this amazing connection when I was led to 'accidentally' discover the work of Frederic Myers, and was able to verify the similarity between his information and my own experience.

Other reports from the spirit world tell of souls going to a sort of staging area when they first pass over. They are then directed by a thought process to finally link up with their spirit family, with each family group residing in their own cluster community. Souls here are not seen as forms but as orbs of light. However, they are able to manifest a recognisable image resembling their human form. These orbs are now being witnessed and recorded in large numbers all over the world with the aid of digital photography. Several such photographs were taken in Brazil during my stay at the Casa, and I witnessed dozens of orbs as they surrounded John of God in the gardens there at twilight.

Certain belief systems equate the various planes of existence to the bodies in the solar system as they perceived it. According to the Kabbalah, the first dimension is the earth, the second dimension is the moon, the third dimension is Mercury, the fourth dimension is Venus, the fifth dimension is the Sun, the sixth dimension is Mars, the seventh dimension is Jupiter, the eighth dimension is Saturn, the ninth dimension is represented by the zodiac, and the tenth dimension is represented by the fixed stars.

The renowned author and psychic Edgar Cayce, referred to as 'the sleeping prophet', channelled similar information. According to Cayce, our experience relates to the universe rather than just a localised area. Each solar system is like a university, with many dimensions of learning available, through which we must travel. Our solar system has nine dimensions or planes of consciousness, the earth being the third.

The Monroe Institute Gateway program, based on studies into out-of-body experiences, has identified several different levels which it calls 'Focus points'.[2] The studies suggest these focus points start very close to the earth. They are the beginning of a journey through different levels of consciousness, where over time we can reflect on our own spiritual journey, and also make contact with guides and others in spirit. It seems to me that this describes the location many of us go to in deep meditation and inner reflection.

Not all levels of reality beyond earth are closed to us while we're still in physical form. Focus 21 is inhabited by people still in their physical bodies in the dream state, in delirium and in other chemically induced states. Focus 23 contains departed souls who have not accepted they have left their body. The belief system territories are in Focus 24, 25 and 26 where non-physical souls are in realities created by their earthly belief systems, similar to what Myers described as the Plane of Illusion. At Focus 27 souls are received into the first layer of the afterlife and treated in a healing centre, before proceeding to other levels. The onward journey then depends on each individual soul and its stage of development.

Even from this brief glance we can see there are different labels for the stages of life after death, just as there are different ways to experience the complexity and enormity of the world of spirit.

8

Where we fit in

*'After your death you will be what you were
before your birth'.*

ARTHUR SCHOPENHAUER, PHILOSOPHER, 1788–1821

In talking about life after death, we are also addressing the question of life before birth. Or to put it another way, life between lives.

It is my belief that eons ago we were separated from the Source of Creation into individual soul energy forms. From there we began the journey home to the Source as our souls evolved. This lifetime is only one small chapter of a very large volume. As the soul is pure energy, it is logical to assume that the Source is also pure energy.

When asked in an interview whether he believed in God, Carl Jung, the eminent psychologist, replied that it was not a matter of believing, but of knowing. While this is very inspiring, most of us still need to have a clear sense of our source.

In an amazing revelation during one meditation I was shown a large ocean with rolling waves and boiling waters. The message came through loud and clear that the Source is actually an ocean of energy, and that each individual is a drop from this vast body. After separation each drop undertakes the great journey, with its own unique experiences, until eventually it is reunited with the Source.

Take a jug of water and remove a cupful—the liquid in both containers still appears the same, even after separation. When the water is poured back into the jug, the two meld into one again. It is impossible to tell the two apart. Ian Lawton describes each soul as being a holographic image of the original source.[1] The nature of holograms is that they can be divided endlessly and still contain every aspect of the original. This suggests we already contain everything needed to become complete. And that's what the Bible means when it refers to mankind being made in the image of God.

So, how does all this work?

Earthly life is like being an actor on the stage. Once we have been cast in a role by spirit, we study and learn all about our designated character, and our relationship with the other characters, before we come to earth. Then, as the cast assembles, it's time to rehearse with our fellow performers under the instructions given by the director. We commit the lines to memory, put on a costume and make-up, and finally we perform for the world at large—we are born on this earthly plane.

After our birth we forget about any performances that came before, as it would be too overwhelming for us to remember all the details. Then at the end of the season, the costumes are returned, the make-up is wiped off for the last time and we, the actors, go home to 'rest'—we return to the spirit world. Then we wait to secure another role on earth. In between roles we may carry out a number of other activities in spirit. Some may even get to go straight into another role.

Actors delve very deeply into the characters they are playing, becoming very familiar with all their psychological aspects and interactions with others. Unfortunately in life we rarely take the opportunity to take a good, hard look at ourselves. Our life actions may even cause distress to others and not impress 'the powers that be' in spirit. This may in turn affect the lessons we have to learn in our next lifetime. All too often we only look deeply at who we are after we arrive back in spirit and have to look back and review the life we have just completed.

How well we performed in our life will influence the next role we are offered. If the director and the audience were not impressed, we may find ourselves out in the cold having to completely rethink our future. We might even end up replaying the same role instead of being offered a new one.

·

What we refer to as death is simply the separation of the soul from the body. The soul—essentially energy—is like a power source for the physical frame it occupies during life. When that power source separates from its body, the soul is freed from its physical limitations.

So, where does it go when cut loose? The newly freed soul suddenly feels a wonderful sense of peace, as all bodily pain and sickness have been released. I have communicated with some people in spirit who could hardly believe the transformation that took place after they left their body. They describe a total sense of freedom and harmony, of leaving all their cares and worries behind them. Suddenly the shackles have been removed as they shed the now unnecessary physical body. I watched my mother's soul pass from her body and this sense of peace and freedom was evident in her face.

My soul mate Judy had a rare heart–lung condition and had been forced to breathe through an oxygen mask for the last few months of her life. She was also bedridden, and for such an active person this was a tragic way to end her life. At her funeral the medium Ruth Wilson saw Judy clearly as she led the coffin procession into the church. She was moving freely and all the frustrations of her last days had disappeared. Ruth said Judy fairly bounced up to the podium to be with me as I delivered the oratory.

I have connected with many people in spirit in the course of my readings for them, and they too have a universal message. They want their loved ones on earth to know they are free of all pain and worry and, most importantly, that they are still very much alive.

Sometimes those in spirit also wish to redress any mistakes they may have made during their lifetime. Several people have come through during my contacts with the afterlife to apologise to members of their family. This usually brings floods of tears from the person left behind, who is still battling to cope with past events. In one memorable experience, Sam was contacted by his father during a group session I was conducting. His father was most insistent that I pass on a message. He was begging for forgiveness for having treated his son so badly when he was growing up. Sam, who was a pretty tough bloke, broke down at this point, overcome by hearing an apology from his father.

Of course, those souls who leave their body suddenly in accidents or unexpected circumstances may have a different reaction, as they often feel confused and uncertain. Some souls refuse to accept that they are 'dead', stubbornly reject all help and choose to stay earthbound, desperately trying to continue their old life and wondering why nobody takes any notice of them.

Regardless of how we die or why we refuse to move on, we are all met and helped by spirit 'counsellors', whether they are family, friends or guides, who explain our transition. The spirit world does not give up on any soul and gives us many opportunities to cross over if we are earthbound, as well as to work our way through the planes. However, as with all things spirit, it is a matter of free will and so some souls take longer than others to accept their transition. All souls eventually return to their Source as they resolve their issues and progress along their journey.

9

Is suicide punished?

As we get into the detail about life after death, there are so many aspects to consider. Perhaps one of the most concerning is that of suicide. And for those who are left behind on earth, the question of what happens to those who commit suicide is a sensitive one.

There is no black and white answer. Some souls do indeed go to a special sphere for reflection and re-education, while others go to different areas of the lower astral for their soul growth. While nobody is punished, the souls of people who suicide usually return to the earth after counselling to re-learn their lessons. So while they may feel they are escaping earthly tests by taking their own life, in the long run they still have to confront their unresolved issues as part of their soul growth. While we are given free will, dishonouring the contract for one's life is not to be taken lightly.

The lower astral is divided into many sections, and souls are placed here according to their circumstances and development. Deepak Chopra asserts that there are actually two main areas of the astral plane, which is divided into upper and lower regions.[1] The lower astral regions harbour ghosts, disembodied souls and spirits that for one reason or another are 'stuck'.

Lobsang Rampa in his book *I Believe* describes the lower astral experience very graphically.[2] His central character, Algenon, finds himself in a dark, misty place, feeling abandoned and alone after committing suicide. Gradually unseen voices penetrate his thoughts, offering to help him. First he has to admit to himself that there is, in fact, life after death. The voices tell him that he is surrounded by black clouds of doubt and unreason, which he has created for himself, and only he can destroy. When he demands some kind of proof of this, a break appears in the black clouds, but then closes again as his negativity takes over.

Eventually Algenon gives in and asks for help to move beyond this bleak place. The black clouds grow lighter and fade into a light mist and Algenon then sees he is accompanied by a shadowy figure which emerges from the gloom. It is a friendly man in a yellow robe, welcoming him to his new life. As the clouds clear, Algenon realises he has actually been standing on 'the greenest of green grass and the air around him was vibrant with life, pulsating with energy'. He also feels the energy of music in the air, and realises he was surrounded by people all the time, even though he had believed he was alone. People in deep depression, described by Winston Churchill as 'the black dog', can relate to this situation I am sure.

Rampa's book was created as a work of fiction, but like his 18 other books, it included information channelled from spirit and gives some remarkable insights into the mysteries of life and the afterlife.

Rampa was a real enigma in his own life. He was a Cornish plumber whose body was allegedly taken over by the spirit of a former Tibetan lama, bringing about a huge change in the life of this simple man. Rampa writes how one day the spirit appeared and asked him to honour the agreement made before his birth to allow the lama's spirit to take over his body. The plumber's spirit apparently left soon after, and the lama took its place. Suddenly this simple Cornish man revealed immense knowledge of Tibetan Buddhism, including their mystic rites, as well as detailed recollections of China and Tibet.

Rampa's works remain controversial to this day, but the details they contain give plenty of food for thought.

10

Staying for your own funeral

A lovely friend of mine, Rachel, knowing that her life was fading, chose to spend her last weeks meditating and preparing for the next part of her journey. She asked her friends to respect her privacy so that she could focus all her strength on this preparation. Rachel was a beautiful and vivacious woman in her late fifties. She embraced life fully, and I felt very sad when I received the news she was gone. Her funeral was another story altogether.

Surrounded by her grieving family and friends, I was delighted to make contact with Rachel. I felt her presence quite clearly early in the service even before I saw her spirit. She was so happy to be rid of her cancer-ravaged body. During the funeral I actually saw her dancing down the aisle looking vital and beautiful once again.

When Rachel contacted me during the service she told me how free she felt. I was also able to give various messages to some of her close friends about her new energy and her vital appearance. This was very comforting to them after seeing her suffer so much. I was then reminded by a mutual friend that Rachel had always loved dancing and used to conduct dance workshops, so it was apt that I saw her dancing at her own funeral. There was no doubt a new door had opened for her.

Rachel and I had known each other for many years. She had been the catalyst for my spiritual awareness to commence when we were both very young. We were appearing in a stage production of *Daughter of Silence* in the early 1960s. Rachel was the star of the show and I was playing a small role. I was very smitten by this beautiful girl, so when she asked me if I would like to go to a spiritualist church with her, I eagerly accepted. At the time I would probably have accompanied her to a bikie gang rally I was so infatuated!

The spiritualist meeting was the first I had ever attended and it had a big impact on me. I realised for the first time in my life that contact with the spirit world was possible. My mind and intuition had been opened. The medium stood on a small platform in front of the congregation. One by one, along each row of the audience, the medium passed appropriate messages to everyone present. From their reactions I knew the messages were genuine.

Rachel was given reassurance from a friend who had died tragically in a motorbike accident, which brought tears to her eyes. I remember being given a very encouraging message about my future and being told that I was 'one in a million', which was very surprising. Rachel thought it was just letting me know I was only one of many. Maybe it was my ego, but I chose to take the other interpretation at the time and that message has provided inspiration for me ever since.

Through my association with the spiritualist church, and with my own numerous experiences over time, I've come to realise just how alive the dead are. The details of their journey are fascinating and offer us lots of clues to what life is like on the other side.

It seems many souls want to stay with their loved ones until after their funeral, and before beginning their journey back into the world of spirit. There is often a lot of concern felt by the deceased for those left behind, particularly if their loved ones are deeply grieving for them. And sometimes souls are still in a state of confusion at the time of their funeral, not fully realising they have died.

The evolution of the soul itself plays an important part in what happens next. Advanced souls, once freed from their physical body, intuitively remember where they are heading. They waste no time in hanging around once they have completed their earthly life's work. However, some people are so sick and weak they need help from those in spirit to make their transition, as this too requires energy. Others can become very confused after long illnesses or extended medication. Like most of us going on a major trek, we want to rest up, so we can get the most out of it. Rachel knew intuitively she was close to death and chose to spend her final days resting peacefully.

Spirit helpers are always there waiting to assist us in our crossing. Family members and other loved ones who have gone on before us know when we are about to cross over and are waiting to welcome us home again. Help is always on hand. It is up to us to accept it.

Sometimes family and close friends report brief contact in some way with the person who has just 'died'. They may experience a strong *feeling*, a familiar perfume or fragrance, or hear unusual sounds, while others actually *see* the departed, or receive symbolic signs. This apparently depends both on the soul itself and those who are open to contact.

There are many ways those we love communicate with us. For example, we may hear their favourite music in unexpected places. When my partner Judy passed over, I kept hearing the song I associated with her being played on radio for months afterwards. Several times I had to pull over and stop the car as I fought back tears. I still have an emotional reaction when I hear Joe Cocker's 'You Are So Beautiful'.

The size and nature of the funeral can make it difficult for contact during the service. When Judy died I was asked to give the funeral oration, as nobody else felt strong enough to do it. This was the hardest speech I have ever made and, at the time, I wondered how I was going to be able to speak without breaking down. Fortunately, Ruth Wilson had given me a beautiful text to read to the congregation, so I had something to hold, to steady my trembling hands. When I reached the pulpit I felt a burst of strength come to me from somewhere, which gave me the ability to speak confidently. Ruth later told me that when I started to speak Judy suddenly appeared beside me and held my arm. She was able to witness the powerful impact Judy's support had on me. Even though Judy did not always want to be the centre of attention, this felt right, and I'm sure she would have wanted to join in on the proceedings.

Several years after that, Michael, a friend and colleague, had a well-attended funeral at a large city theatre and, try as I might, I was not able to sense his presence there. Later I did connect with him at the wake, which was held at his beloved home, and was aware that he was circulating among the guests. Michael was always a wonderful host and I feel sure he appreciated this occasion to be with those he loved.

People do not always get to attend their own funerals. Another friend of mine, Olga, who had worked in TV and was one of life's real characters, passed over early in 2009 after a stroke had left her debilitated and wasting away over many months. I could not feel her presence at the funeral and when I later asked my guide M, he told me that she was too weak after her passing and had gone straight into recuperation in the spirit world. A pity, really, as it was one of the best funerals I have ever been to, with some wonderful speakers. Olga would have loved being the centre of attention one last time.

11

Accepting we are dead

Some souls do not at first realise they have indeed 'died' and cannot understand why people don't take any notice of them, ignoring all attempts at communication. In other cases souls can be weighed down by the excessive grief of their family and are unable to separate completely from them, staying around or being pulled back to offer comfort. These souls are often described as being 'earthbound' and can stay attached to the earth for varying amounts of time.

Some souls feel they have unfinished business and try to interfere in the lives of those they've left behind. This can be done in a spirit of helpfulness, but is often disturbing for those still living. Others hang around because they fear that their activities during life will see them issued with a one-way ticket to hellfire and brimstone.

Edgar Cayce, the famous psychic, believed some souls come to terms with this confusion and gain satisfaction by merging with the energy they can tap into amongst those still living. These souls live vicariously through the various emotions and mental activities surrounding them. Some try to meddle in things that no longer concern them, by influencing people's thoughts through dreams and the like, while others even try to take over the body of someone they are trying to control. Sudden and complete changes of personality in a person can often indicate this kind of influence.

People on earth who are addicted to such things as alcohol, drugs and sex are particularly vulnerable to these meddlesome spirits. As an addiction can offer an entry point for a discarnate spirit, problems of this kind are the first conditions to be addressed. Specialised counselling can often help, but it is still the responsibility of the person affected to address the situation. Society is often all too willing to dismiss such symptoms as a mental condition.

Psychic readers and healers can often attract unwanted energies and even have negative entities attach themselves. Special clearing is needed to free yourself from this influence.

12

Possession and 'walk-ins'

Some spirits are believed to be able to take over the body of someone they are trying to control. This is known by various names including 'possession' and 'walk-in'.

There is another situation where two souls supposedly agree to swap places in a body for the mutual development of each. The first soul moves on, while the new soul takes the person in a whole new direction in life. This is a very old belief stemming from the Hindu faith that has found new popularity in recent times, especially with soul energies from 'aliens' wanting to become part of life on earth.

Interest in the 'walk-in' phenomenon was stimulated a few decades back by the popular *Seth Speaks* series of books written by trance medium Jane Roberts. Roberts described Seth as an energy personality who spoke through her while her own consciousness temporarily left her body. Ruth

Montgomery then wrote *Strangers Among Us*, a collection of accounts of walk-ins, which included prominent historical figures among her subjects. One of these was Thomas Jefferson, who was thought to have hosted walk-in spirits who wrote the US Declaration of Independence.

One of my most fascinating interviews on my radio show was with Jason Andrews, who had a very troubled childhood, full of strange dreams and weird experiences. It turned out that Jason had been abducted by aliens as a child, and as he grew into adolescence realised he was in fact a soul whose home was elsewhere. Jason has amazing psychic and healing powers, which he uses in a very everyday fashion, choosing to live life as a normal human being. There are many such people as Jason in our midst, and they have now been dubbed 'Star Children'.

I put the question of walk-ins to my guide M, who explained that what we call soul transfer is actually more like an overlay of soul energy. In most cases the higher self, sometimes referred to as the overself, transfers some of its spiritual energy to a certain person. This has the effect of inspiring that person and often transforming them in some way. He said that sometimes an advanced soul can step in to replace the original soul, but it is very rare.

This would explain the stories of personal transformations that we hear about after near-death experiences. Most people who have had a near-death experience say that they return with a very different attitude to life, and most add that they have also lost all fear of death.

This stepping aside process isn't all that uncommon. Unconscious mediums have learned to 'step aside' to allow a spirit to come through to communicate their messages. While I personally find this practice not to my liking, I've witnessed some amazing contacts.

Probably the most famous medium in this field is J.Z. Knight, who channels the spirit of Ramtha. I have watched J.Z. transform from a very feminine woman to take on the energy of an ancient warlord from Atlantean times. It was a fascinating experience for the large audience present to witness her energy change from the feminine to that of a powerful warrior king. J.Z. is able to hold the warlord's commanding energy for long periods of time without wavering. The transition back to her feminine self is visible evidence of the vast difference in the two 'personas'.

So while we may imagine life in the spirit world is well ordered and fairly straightforward, it is actually far more detailed and at times more fluid than we may think.

Part B
The Journey Home

13

The tunnel linking both worlds

From the many accounts from people who have had near-death experiences, the journey home to the spirit world usually involves travelling through a tunnel. It's a kind of inter-dimensional worm hole linking the two worlds. During the near-death experience, these people glimpsed the spirit world, and some were given the option to stay and others were told to go back and complete their life's mission.

Physical death is not just one specific moment at the end of our life. Medically speaking it is a process that begins when the heart stops beating, the lungs stop working and the brain ceases functioning. This takes anywhere from a few seconds to an hour or more and is the stage where near-death experiences may also occur.

Near-death experiences have been widely documented. Experts such as Dr Raymond Moody and Dr Cherie

Sutherland have written in depth about them. In fact Cherie told me near-death experiences are not a recent phenomenon. They can be traced back many hundreds of years. She researched a story told by the Venerable Bede as far back as the eighth century. Drythelm, a devout Northumbrian, 'died' after a severe illness and came back to life the next day, much to his family's amazement. He told his wife not to be afraid as he had come back from the dead and now had to live his life in a very different way. Cherie maintains those who return do change their lives dramatically after being given a second chance, and has many case studies to bear this out.

Dr Harry Oldfield, a pioneer of Kirlian photography (photographing the aura) as a medical research tool in the UK and abroad, told me about his own near-death experience. Harry—who describes himself as an 'inventor, scientist, thinker and somewhat eccentric seeker after new and forgotten knowledge, and an explorer of undiscovered realms'—has been researching his theories about life and its meaning for more than two decades. Harry is one of that rare breed of scientist who is able to keep an open mind about unusual and unexplained phenomena. His inventions and research work in these areas are slowly being accepted by the scientific community.

While Harry has a bubbly personality and wicked sense of humour, he became very serious as he recounted his near-death experience. During a period when he lived alone, he went to bed one night as normal and experienced what seemed to him like a dream. He described going through 'a foggy sort of tunnel' and in the distance saw a whole lot of familiar faces, including his deceased father. As he approached, his father waved him back the way he had come. At that moment Harry's cat started howling loudly from somewhere behind him. Harry was quite surprised at this because his cat was also dead. The noise woke him and he sat bolt upright in bed.

As Harry sat there trying to make sense of what he thought was a dream, he realised there was a strange smell in the house. When he went to investigate he found a gas leak coming from under the stairwell. By now he was feeling sick but managed to stagger outside, where he collapsed on the front lawn. Somehow Harry gathered enough strength to call the fire brigade, who turned up a few minutes later. The fire chief told him the gas leak was so intense that if he hadn't been woken up, he would have died. Harry's impish sense of humour returned and he told me straight-faced, 'I wasn't game enough to tell them my dead cat woke me!'

In a personal reading, David, a man in his late forties, told me his story about leaving his body while recuperating in a hospital ward. As he watched the medical staff attend to his physical form, he was suddenly joined by the spirit of the man in the bed next to him. They exchanged silent greetings and David then watched his neighbour's spirit disappear out through the hospital roof. Returning to his body David later regained consciousness and told the hospital staff of his experience. They were amazed at this information and confirmed that the second man had indeed died.

Ian McCormack, a former 'surfie' from New Zealand, told my radio audience the story of his amazing near-death experience. While surfing as a young man in Sri Lanka, Ian was stung by six box jellyfish. The sting from just one of these creatures can be fatal unless treated immediately. Ian was rushed to hospital unconscious and had his first contact with an unseen spiritual force as he was being transported in the ambulance. He was shown visions of several men who had hurt him in the past and a voice asked if he could forgive them. At first he refused, but then he asked the unseen voice, 'If I forgive those men, will "God" forgive me for my dissolute life?'

Arriving at the hospital Ian found himself floating on the roof of the operating room. Before this Ian had travelled extensively through the East and studied yoga and other spiritual practices, so he understood the concept of his spirit leaving his body and astral travelling. He felt he was dying and 'going on a one-way trip', as the toxins in his body had left him completely paralysed. Ian was then taken on an amazing journey.

After a frightening trip through a dark plane, where spirit voices told him he was in hell, Ian was drawn up by a beam of light and through a tunnel where he was bathed in a pure white light. Ian found himself communicating with the light and eventually connected with what he now believes is the Source of Creation. Suddenly a stream of unconditional love filled his entire being, which he felt, at the time, was undeserved. Then a figure in white robes of pure light came forward and welcomed him with outstretched hands. Ian described the light shining from the stranger's face enveloping him in the purest energy imaginable. Feeling that the innocence of a child had been restored to him, Ian looked into what he still believes was 'the face of God'. Moving closer, he felt a state of holiness come into his own being, then noticed the outstretched hands had unmistakable marks of crucifixion on them and realised it was Jesus who was greeting him.

As the figure of light turned, a portal opened up behind him revealing, as Ian described it, 'an entire new eternity and a kind of new earth. There were crystal clear streams, flowers, trees and rolling green hills, but no people. It was like an untouched garden—a paradise. There was also a new heaven above this new earth.'

Gazing about him Ian felt such a sense of belonging, he wondered why he hadn't been born there in the first place. He was told if he wanted to be part of that world, he would have to be reborn. He then realised his experience in the ambulance was in effect a rebirth after he asked for and also gave forgiveness. This being of light then offered Ian the choice of staying in paradise or returning to earth. Ian was about to tell the figure that he wanted to stay when he looked over his shoulder and saw an image of his mother standing in the tunnel. He realised the love she had for him and what his death would mean to her, so reluctantly he decided to return to his pain-ravaged body.

Ian's life changed dramatically after his recovery. Now with his wild surfie days behind him he has been travelling extensively sharing his experiences with a wide range of audiences.

Stories abound of people leaving their body and floating around the ceiling as they watch their body undergoing medical procedures in hospital. These recollections come from those who have decided or been told to return to earth. Interestingly, they all report life is never the same for them again. Hamish Miller, for example, had a near-death experience that changed the course of his life. He decided to leave behind his successful business, going on to become one of Britain's best-known and most highly respected dowsers. During the 1980s and 90s, he undertook journeys across England and New Zealand, and from Ireland to Israel, tracking down ancient ley lines and sacred sites.

Another interesting point is that the journey through the tunnel to the next world is described in similar terms by people from different walks of life. Regardless of race or religion, a common experience is the initial feeling of peace in separating from the body which remains behind as they float through the tunnel towards a distant light. Some souls are turned back at the point of entry into the other world by a spiritual being, while others enter a world of light where they are met by deceased friends and relatives, before being told it is not their time and they must go back. Some are also given the choice of staying or returning to earth.

Those who do return, often reluctantly, lose any fear of death they may have had prior to this. They speak strongly of the existence of an afterlife and often embrace the concept of reincarnation. The 'being' they encounter is usually described as a being of light, or perhaps religious figures that correspond with their beliefs. The experience is highly emotional and like a rebirth in many ways. Sadly, many who have had a near-death experience are reluctant to talk about it, because it is a sacred experience and they don't want it to be ridiculed. Fortunately that, too, is changing as more people come forward and feel confident enough to tell their story.

Those who have near-death experiences can sometimes provide inspiring messages for others on their return. American writer Diane Goble recounts the message she was given, to make death a *part* of life and not the *end* of life.[1] She was asked to share this message with those she contacted. Diane maintains that we need to talk about death, get comfortable with it, to prepare ourselves and our loved ones for our departure. She was told we can expect reunions with those we love at the end of our physical lives, and that in fact we will meet again, many times, in many places. I read a lovely story once saying that when a baby is born the angels weep to lose one of their own, but when a person comes home to spirit there is much celebration. In life here we react in exactly the opposite way.

It appears not everybody has the tunnel experience, even though they have left their body. Writer and artist Trypheyna McShane, had a near-death experience after she collapsed at home and woke in hospital some hours later.[2] She found herself floating around the ceiling, looking down at medical staff frantically trying to resuscitate the woman she could see in a bed below her. She felt a wonderful sense of peace and contentment and was in no way concerned for her situation. After a while Trypheyna was shocked to recognise the body in the bed was her own. She passed out again and when she woke she was back in her body. A doctor came in to tell her how serious her condition was, but she didn't need to worry as they had new drugs to help heal her. Trypheyna, now feeling composed and filled with a new sense of purpose, told him she was going to heal herself and didn't want the drugs. The doctor was less than impressed, but Trypheyna made a full recovery.

The vast majority of accounts of near-death experiences are glowing and positive. It is very rare to hear reports of people being confronted by the kind of dark visions that Ian McCormack experienced. I have heard accounts of people who separated from their body and found themselves drawn up and away from earth, sometimes describing it as like falling up, not down. They then found themselves in a place like a large park or open space with someone waiting to greet them. Other spirits tell of simply waking up in the afterlife after losing consciousness when they 'died'. These accounts were from those who lived on earth many years ago in much simpler times. Their spiritual experiences reflect their daily lives at the time. It may also be that the tunnel experience happened to them while they were 'asleep' to help them with their transition. Now that we live in an age of computers and other technological advances, some of us may expect our journey home to spirit to be more like going through a worm hole in a science fiction film.

As I started this book, my guide M told me that I would be given a series of experiences which would show what happened to me in between lives. While visiting Brazil soon after this I was offered two very special crystals while attending the healing centre run by John of God at the Casa de Dom Inácio. These crystals, which are each about the size of a very large coffee mug, were mined deep in the earth in Brazil. The energy that comes from merely holding these crystals is extremely powerful and at first made me dizzy to even touch them. When I carried my new crystals in a small bag from the Casa back to my lodgings, every stray dog in the neighbourhood came rushing up to me with tails wagging, jumping up at the crystals. These same dogs had studiously avoided me for the previous week or so. I found my meditations at the Casa took on a whole new meaning after that, because I was able to reach greater depths, often leaving the body and connecting with beings in higher dimensions. I am the only person allowed to touch or even see these particular crystals. They are in my possession for the duration of this lifetime and when I pass over they have to be returned to the sea or a lake.

Every time I meditate with the crystals, time stands still for me and I am taken on incredible journeys of the spirit. What feels like a short meditation often turns out to be well over an hour or more. During the course of these meditations my guide M came to me and took me back to my death in my previous lifetime in a series of visions, so I could recount my experiences after leaving the body.

14

Last time around

So what of Brian, the young soldier, my former self? His unit was advancing on the enemy trenches when he was ripped apart by a stream of bullets from a German machine gunner. He was hit in the chest and also his right side, around his waist area. While collapsing to the ground he was also injured in the head around his left eye. Death did not come immediately. He lay in great pain on the battlefield, while his mates rushed on to tackle the Germans.

Brian called for help, but none came. A great feeling of hopelessness and abandonment engulfed him as his life ebbed away. He felt that his mates had deserted him, and he was alone and frightened. With no understanding of what was happening to him, Brian was a desolate and miserable figure. He lay in agony for an hour before finally dying.

Then something strange occurred. At first not realising he was 'dead', Brian got up and wandered the battlefield.

By now he was in a confused state, looking desperately for his unit, which he couldn't find. Even though he was no longer in pain, he felt even more abandoned than before. Then, suddenly, seemingly out of nowhere, his grandmother appeared alongside him. Now, more confused than ever, Brian was immediately concerned for her safety—battlefields are no place for little old ladies. 'Gran, what are you doing here?' he stammered. 'You're not supposed to be here. Get down before the Germans see you.'

His grandmother just smiled, shook her head, then motioned for him to follow her. After a few moments he did so, mainly because he had no other idea what else to do. It was then Brian remembered his grandmother had passed away a few years before the war began; he was still at school at the time. Suddenly he realised—he must be dead, too. His grandmother nodded as if she could read his thoughts, smiling because she knew he finally understood.

She held out her hand, and feeling dazed he took it in his. As they wandered away from the battlefield, the sounds of fighting faded away and the light began to dim as if night was falling. They went through a gate shaped like a three-pointed star, and entered a tunnel where they started moving faster and faster. Brian remembered a train ride he had as a boy that went through a long tunnel and this felt the same, but when he looked around they were not in a carriage—their bodies just seemed to float in space.

There was a whooshing sound as they started to go even faster, and a galaxy of lights flashed by them. Brian held on tightly to Gran's hand, as it was a strange and unnerving experience for him. Then, without warning, they burst into bright sunlight.

When his eyes adjusted Brian thought he was back in Devon, England. They arrived at what seemed like a railway station, got into a trap pulled by a pony, and drove through the countryside. When they paused for a rest under the shade of a tree, Brian looked across the countryside of rolling green hills to the sea in the distance and, feeling contented and at peace, dozed off. They resumed their journey in the cart and eventually arrived at what felt to Brian like his village in Devon, with familiar houses and several faces he recognised. They were all smiling at him. He felt like he was home again.

Inside his grandmother's house there was a big fruit cake on the kitchen table and a large pot of tea. Brian was glad he'd had a chance to rest under that tree and get himself together as there were several people waiting to greet him and his welcome home provided quite a few surprises. He somehow recognised his 'sister' who welcomed him with open arms. It took Brian a little while to remember that he did not have a sister back on earth. As he stared at her she reminded him of a past life they had shared, and said it would all become clear soon. Observing from the sidelines

I also recognised my son Matt from this current lifetime. Even though his appearance was different, I knew from the sense of his energy it was Matt.

Then, a real surprise. Two army mates came over to Brian with big grins on their faces. There was Tosh, the big cockney, and Larry, a much smaller bloke, who had both died before Brian, and they told him they had been waiting for him to come over. The final surprise was being welcomed by Captain Osbourne, Brian's commanding officer, who, unlike many other officers, had always treated the men very decently. Brian jumped up to salute, but Osbourne laughed and told him all that was behind them now. It was a great reunion. Even if they did only have tea to drink!

After a while Brian started to feel overwhelmed by the very happy, noisy tea party, so everybody said goodbye and left him to rest. It was only then that he started to worry about his family back on earth, so he asked his grandmother about his wife Jenny and his little son Simon. She told him not to worry, explaining that if he wished, he would be able to go back and visit them later, when his strength returned. As Brian was feeling exhausted now, Gran showed him to a room where he could recover.

•

The next chapter in my previous life came during another hypnotherapy session several months later. As I returned to my present consciousness, I was still feeling a little stunned that I could split myself between two realities—my life in the 21st century and my life as a World War I soldier. Yet the more I thought about it, the more I could feel the different emotions, the different bodies, the very different life situations. It was all too real to be a dream. But there's always that part of you that doubts.

After this regression, I thought long and hard about this wartime experience I witnessed. I knew that we don't relive past experiences unless they are relevant to our present situation. When past issues resurface, we experience again the emotional pain, the physical problems and all the other issues related to what we went through. As I sifted through these experiences several aspects of my current life also started to make sense.

I had been born with a problem in my right side, so much so that I'd had a hernia operation at two years of age. It was my right side that had been badly hurt during battle. In my present life I also had a lazy muscle in my eye at birth and had to wear glasses at an early age. You guessed it, the problem was in the left eye, which had been injured as Brian fell to the ground wounded a lifetime ago. Fortunately I was given a spiritual operation on my left eye through John of God, the Brazilian medium who works with a team of doctors in spirit to heal people. Now I no longer need to wear glasses except for reading. My eyes have also straightened.

An extreme case of eczema had erupted over 80 per cent of my body after seeing John of God two years previously in New Zealand. I had asked him to 'release the past'. Interestingly, the worst of the eczema was in my right side where my guide showed me Brian had been mortally wounded. During that operation in Brazil I experienced some very real sensations as the doctors in spirit worked to heal me. This included a sharp pain, like a red hot needle being jabbed into my right side. I was also told to meditate deeply and open my heart to allow the healing to take place. The eczema which had been plaguing me for the previous two years finally started to clear. I began to completely release and heal the past.

My guide M told me I was fortunate to see Brian being escorted through the tunnel as my spiritual understanding in that life as Brian was in its infancy. Perhaps this was because Brian had killed other men and was then slain in a horrible war while still so young. Either that or previous soul experiences were taken into account.

The pieces of the puzzle kept coming together. I had a lifelong fascination with World War I, and in particular the Western Front, but I was born in 1942 so it would probably have been more appropriate for me to have had an interest in World War II. I knew that Brian had lived in Devon and was part of the Devonshire Regiment, but I had always thought the big battles of the Somme were in 1917. Research proved the major battles were actually fought in 1916 when the big British and French advance was made. When I tried to find out about his army regiment my initial research came up blank and I started to have some doubts about what I'd seen. Then one winter's afternoon M's voice came into my thoughts telling me to switch on the TV and watch the History Channel. I found myself watching a program called *The Battle of the Somme*.

The documentary gave me a very strange, unsettled feeling as I experienced a sense of déjà vu. I was stunned to hear a reference to the 2nd Devonshire Regiment. This was my regiment! It had played a key part in that July battle and suffered great casualties around Mametz. So it *had* happened. My doubts were put to rest.

A stone plaque erected at the entrance to the Devonshire Regiment's Cemetery at Mametz reads—'The 8th and 9th Devons suffered very heavy casualties as they left their forward trench to attack. Later that day the survivors buried their fallen comrades in that same trench and erected a wooden memorial with the words which are carved in the cross above: 'The Devonshires held this trench. The Devonshires hold it still.'

Past-life researchers always take note of a person's fascination with a particular time or event in history, as it is a good indication you may have experienced a lifetime there. I have long been fascinated with ancient Egypt and Rome, and other past-life regressions have revealed that I had lives in those periods of history as well.

One regression revealed I was a Roman soldier sent to Egypt as part of the invading force. I was the son of a senator and was murdered by a jealous woman in Cairo. Apparantly I was ordered back to Rome and had no intention of taking her with me, which triggered her rage. Shortly before this regression I had visited Cairo and experienced a real fear for my life. I was very puzzled as there was no good reason for this at the time. But, as often happens, past-life regressions tap into our spirit and reveal a very good reason for our fears and fascinations.

15

Experiences in the tunnel

The tunnel experience has been verified by many people under hypnosis who have been regressed to their own previous time of passing. Most report a kind of pulling sensation as their soul leaves their body. This is followed by a great sense of freedom and relief from pain and suffering. My late partner Judy described a sensation of having hands extended from spirit that gently helped her slip from her body.

At this point some people head straight for the tunnel, while others choose to stay around to comfort loved ones in their grief. Most of the time family and friends are too upset to receive the messages of comfort that the departed soul is trying to communicate. It can be a frustrating time for liberated souls as they desperately try to let their loved ones know they are not dead but still with them. Sadly nobody sees or hears them. Those who have passed over are feeling not only unshackled from the chains of their physical body, but experiencing a huge expansion of energy as their spiritual form becomes free from all restrictions.

I was comforting Anna, a close friend of mine, after the passing of her mother earlier that day, when I heard a voice clearly coming through in my thoughts. Anna's mother was trying to let her daughter know she was there in the room with her, but she got me instead. When I acknowledged her presence, I heard her clearly say, 'Thank God someone can hear me.' She went on to provide evidence it was really her, giving Anna some intimate details that had meaning only to them. I had never met Anna's mother, so simply passed on the messages. My friend was so relieved that her mother was not completely lost to her, while her mother's departed soul was no longer frustrated at being ignored.

As mentioned earlier, many souls stay around for their own funeral offering comfort to the mourners before they finally feel able to move to the tunnel to start their new life. It appears if we have the energy we are usually given the choice of whether to attend our own funeral. Most souls take the opportunity. I suppose many of us would want to be at our own funeral, even if it was just to see who turned up on the day!

An important point to remember is that there is always someone there to meet us shortly after we leave the body. Our helpers in the world of spirit have been given notice of our impending arrival home, although the time can be flexible and those in the spirit world can not always know the exact moment of our arrival, as is the case with some accidents. Modern intervention styles of medicine can obviously play a part in this, too, as it seems we are all reluctant to let our loved ones go and dose them up with drugs or keep them in comas. As there is no time in the non-physical world, this can also be a factor.

So, how do those in spirit know we'll soon be joining them? The answer is unclear. There is evidence from contact with the spirit world that we do have a destiny and a time limit on each life. There is also the possibility that the imminently departing soul sends out its own signal knowing that it will soon be returning home. However, if a person passes over prior to the other members of their family, or they do not yet have any friends on the other side, they are still met. A special guide is appointed to perform a meet-and-greet service and help them settle into their new life. So when we do cross over it is comforting to know that we are expected and there are no embarrassing moments from those on the other side, such as 'Hello, who are you, what are you doing here?'

16

The final moments

My grandfather Harry Smith passed over when I was a young teenager. Harry was a man of the land, who called a spade a spade. As a young boy I loved spending time with him. He was an inspiration for me in many ways. While he was a wonderful family man with very high ethics, he was not religious. Nor did he ever speak to me about any spiritual matters. He was more like a life coach, I guess. As a young boy I called him Pop, but in recent years we reconnected on a different basis.

In the last hours leading up to his death, Harry was bedridden and the family gathered round to say their farewells. He drifted in and out of consciousness and appeared to be speaking with his mother and his sisters, who had all passed over many years before. At the end he sat up and described a magnificent staircase opening up in front of him. Then he uttered the phrase that still lives with me to this day: 'We know nothing.' With that he sank back on his pillows and passed from this life.

The appearance of people from the spirit world who visit when someone is near death seems to vary according to the individual's experience. Spirits are apparently able to appear to the returning soul in a form that is instantly recognisable to them, even if it is not a photographic image of that person as they were in their last life. Perhaps, like me, you have had a dream of a departed loved one and the next day you remember it in vivid detail, but on deeper recollection you realise they appeared 'different' than how you remembered them. Just how different is always difficult to explain, but whatever the case you instantly recognised them in your dream.

Dreams are a very common way of communicating with those in spirit and while the more sceptical dismiss such dreams, there is plenty of evidence to prove otherwise. We will look more deeply at communication with those who have passed in later chapters.

There are many instances of deceased friends and relatives visiting people just prior to their passing, so in some cases the reception committee in the afterlife is not always completely unexpected. Those left behind often disregard this as merely hallucinations brought about by sickness or the ramblings of old age, yet trance channel and medium Marcia Quinton has worked as a nurse for most of her life and has seen many people preparing to leave their bodies. She says it is very common at this time for people to have conversations with departed souls who have come to give support and help prepare them for their transition.

So, despite our fears to the contrary, we never really die alone. Most departed souls are only too pleased to leave the cares and worries of earthly life behind them once they find themselves in such peaceful, loving surroundings and are ready to proceed on the next stage of their journey.

17

Healing time

'Healing is a matter of time, but it is sometimes
also a matter of opportunity.'

HIPPOCRATES, PHILOSOPHER, 460 BCE–370 BCE

When we pass over, all of us need some form of healing from situations we experienced during our earthly life. For example, the spirit of Brian, my former self, went to the afterlife bearing the scars of war and all its horrors.

Our soul does not automatically become instantly pure when it returns to the world of spirit. When our soul leaves the body behind to begin the journey home, it still bears the imprint of the life it has just completed. This may include mental, physical or emotional scarring. If a person has suffered a long illness, died suddenly, or was in any kind of stress or emotional upheaval at the time of passing, the shock of this is firmly imprinted on the astral body that returns to spirit. This explains some accounts from deceased souls who suddenly 'wake up' and find themselves in an unfamiliar setting.

Other contributing factors to the traumas we carry with us can include the effects of overindulgence in such activities as drug-taking, smoking, drinking or gambling, as well as the emotional scars created over our lifetime. The extent of our trauma is a reflection of all we have experienced up until that point, including any unresolved issues.

So some souls arrive in the afterlife in a state of confusion, while others can be angry because of the circumstances of their passing. Young souls in particular often feel cheated by their early death. Together with those who have passed in dramatic or sudden ways, these disturbed souls are often met by their spirit guide to help settle their emotional state and provide answers for them. Guides patiently explain that whatever the circumstances they experienced around death, it was their time to leave the body and, just like the time of birth, there are no accidents.

Spirits are admitted to a healing centre as soon as possible after their passing to help them cleanse and heal, so they can fully participate in life in the spirit world. From all accounts these healing houses are very similar to hospitals as we understand them, and they range in size and speciality. Some spirits are able to heal in a short period of time while others require an extended treatment period.

Recovery takes place essentially through spiritual healing, with energetic, magnetic and counselling treatments. Doctors in spirit and their assistants treat everyone individually. Each departed soul goes through a period of healing and cleansing at the end of each lifetime, no matter how evolved they may be.

With no concept of earthly time in the afterlife, the duration spent in the healing house will depend on the individual and their state of being. Here, there is no such thing as the passing of *time* as we understand it. To them it may appear as only a few days or weeks, while back on earth months or even years may have passed. This explains why some spirits are able to communicate with us after a short stay in the spirit world, while others do not come through for quite a while.

When I went to Brazil to visit John of God's healing centre, I was given a sudden flash of understanding while in meditation. I was shown that the Casa reflects the healing centre we are taken to just after we arrive back in the spirit world. People come to the Casa from all walks of life and from all around the world for one purpose—healing. Whether that healing is for physical, spiritual, mental or emotional reasons, or a combination of issues, it does not matter. Many languages, reflecting diverse cultures, are heard every day, but everyone is there for the same basic reason. A common bond soon emerges during the healing process, reminding everyone we are all connected, emphasising the universal principle of oneness.

Sometimes healing in the afterlife is immediate and at other times it is just the beginning of a much longer recovery process. Every case is different, everyone's story unique. Some souls experience the centre as a hospital, while others see it more as a clinic or therapy centre. The manifestation will depend on a person's required comfort zone and by what is expected by each individual soul. These healing centres in spirit represent the gateway to a new life. It can truly be said, 'As above, so below.'

18

Inside the healing centre

In my next vision, my guide M showed me Brian being admitted to a special healing house or hospital for British soldiers who had been killed in the war. He told me there were many such hospitals catering for soldiers, sailors and airmen from all the countries participating in that bloody event. Because of the unprecedented carnage, and the huge number of souls crossing over daily, special provisions were required.

The nurse who looked after Brian was named Greta. She was very kind and understanding, and told him she had lived in Switzerland in her last life. First Brian was given a special bath to help 'cleanse' his spirit of the trauma it had just gone through. No water was used. Instead he was bathed in a very soft violet-coloured light. This helped gradually restore Brian's strength, as he was still feeling very weak. The light also helped clear the fuzziness from his head which had accompanied him since his 'death'. Brian was then allocated a bed. While he sensed there were many other soldiers around him, he was still somehow on his own. It was not a private room, but a separate space, almost cocoon like. The doctor in charge was a specialist in military-type spirit hospitals as he was able to relate well to soldiers and their way of life. He told Brian that in his last incarnation he was in the Crimean War, and had devoted his spirit life to looking after soldiers in distress ever since.

Brian's treatment was simply to rest at first, and to have regular 'light baths' to cleanse his spirit. A beam of violet light shone down on him as he lay semi-conscious in his bed. Brian drifted a lot in his thoughts during these treatments. Gradually the memories of his last life on earth began to fade, particularly his terrible recollections of the war. During this time Brian received regular visits from a group of souls who stood around his bed, joined hands and just smiled at him in a loving way. On each occasion he could feel a rush of emotional energy fill his being, and so he looked forward to their visits. No words were ever spoken, but he could feel their loving support. Brian couldn't recall needing or being given any food or drink, but he felt uplifted when Greta attended his bedside.

As his strength started to recover he began to wonder how much longer he would need to stay in hospital. As much as anything he was curious to see what was next.

On one occasion Greta disturbed his reverie, telling him there was someone he needed to see. Almost immediately Brian found himself in a bed in a completely different part of the hospital. When he looked around he saw there was another bed next to him.

With a shock he recognised the sleeping form of Lily, his mother. As far as Brian was concerned, his mother was still alive and well back in England. Greta explained that when she heard the news of her son's death his mother had collapsed. Her other two sons had died earlier in the war and the pain of losing her youngest son as well was simply too much for her.

Brian stayed with his mother for a long time. When she finally awoke, Lily could hardly believe her eyes when she saw her son and the tears started to flow. Lily's spirit doctor had wisely decided that the best form of healing was being reunited with her recently departed son. Lily was still very weak, and they spent what seemed like weeks just lying in adjacent beds, talking and giving spiritual support and love to each other.

Brain and his mother also spoke about his brothers who had been killed earlier in the war. They had been working together as sappers undermining the enemy trenches when a tunnel collapsed and killed them. Their father had been a miner and Brian's brothers were following in his footsteps before war broke out. As he had breathing problems and did not qualify or indeed even have the faintest wish to become a miner, Brian worked in a shop after he left school. Greta came to visit Brian and Lily, even though it was not her ward, and she was able to tell them that the two brothers had recovered and had moved on to the next stage of their life in the spirit world.

Eventually Greta told Brian he was now fully cleansed and able to leave the hospital to rejoin his spiritual family. Brian was a little confused by this as he was already here with his mother. Greta explained that although he had been spending time with his earth mother from his last life, he had another family in spirit, waiting to welcome him home.

Lily was healing rapidly. As Brian prepared to leave the hospital Greta told him he would be able to come back and visit her. As for his brothers, they did visit on one occasion. They were big, burly, very gruff kind of men—nothing like Brian—and Lily was glad to see them, though she enjoyed a special bond with her youngest child. Looking back, Brian felt his and Lily's time together was a very important part of her healing process.

As he left the hospital Brian was happy to be moving on, but he was also sad to leave Greta behind as they had become close friends. Like many young soldiers laid up in hospital he was falling for his nurse.

Having had this detailed experience of my afterlife as Brian, my overall impression of the spirit hospital is that a lot of the healing is done there with loving support. The emphasis of this healing is on restoring our heart energy. I feel it is a form of unconditional love, one of the most powerful forces in the universe.

I also found that after we pass over we each need different degrees of healing. It usually starts with healing showers of energy that cleanse the newly arrived soul from its earthly 'pollution'; rather like having a lovely warm bath or shower after a long journey to refresh our body. The cleansing shower of light is sometimes all a soul requires before continuing its journey in spirit.

The spirit entity Seth, communicating through Jane Roberts, explained the spirit journey like this:

> There is no one after-death reality, but each experience is different. Generally speaking, however, there are dimensions into which these individual experiences will fall. For example, there is an initial stage for those who are still focused strongly in physical reality, and for those who need a period of recuperation and rest. On this level there will be hospitals and rest homes.[1]

Our beliefs can also affect our healing. The beliefs we have created and accepted during our physical life are often so ingrained into our spirit that it takes a long while to undo their effects. When they are first admitted, some patients fail to realise that there is no longer anything wrong with them at all. In some of these cases their 'illness' is overwhelming, because it is embedded in their psyche. These patients are given psychic or spiritual treatments to help them understand their condition is a result of their own beliefs. Those people who are able to pass over with an open heart and an open mind have a far easier journey when they return to the next world. So entering the spirit world it's important to have an open mind.

Brian's return journey was made easier once he accepted his grandmother's presence and put his trust in her.

19

Where to now?

The next stage of my out-of-body experience with my
guide M picked up Brian's afterlife journey as he was
about to leave the healing house.

When we leave these places of healing we are normally
met by our guide or another spirit helper and escorted to
reconnect with our spiritual family. This can be a very
exciting moment. As the world of spirit is so vast, it requires
movement of some type to get back to our soul group. The
family we return to reflects our soul growth, so we go to
that particular area of the spirit world. The wonderful thing
about checking out of this hospital is there are no forms
to fill in, no bills to pay, no administrative hassles. One
moment Brian was inside, and the next he found himself
in the open air sitting under a tree. It was a lot like watching
a film, as one scene dissolved to reveal another.

When Brian looked around, he saw very familiar
surroundings. He found himself on a hilltop, overlooking

the sea a few miles away. Even though he couldn't see the sun, the weather was warm, and the light was very soft. He appeared to be in the countryside near his old home in Devon. But when Brian looked closer, he realised it was a *similar* landscape, but not the same—just familiar enough to give him a feeling of peace and security.

As he gazed into the distance, Brian became aware that somebody was with him. Brian looked up to see the face of an older man looking at him with smiling blue eyes. Dressed in white, his skin appeared dark or well tanned. He was tall and thin with a prominent nose, twinkling eyes and a warm smile. He seemed familiar but Brian could not remember how he knew him.

Brian was immediately given an answer to his puzzled thoughts, even though the man did not move his lips. 'I am Markus, your guide,' the figure said. 'I can answer any questions you may have.'

Markus went on to explain that after Brian's healing time and the ordeal of his wartime experiences, he would be given a chance to rest and recuperate before the next stage of his development. This was to be a kind of holiday.

Shortly afterwards Brian found himself in a village, not unlike the one he had lived in before going to France. A door opened and his grandmother stuck her head out and waved him inside. He went into a reception room where there was a large apple pie with fresh clotted cream, and a big teapot with cups and saucers set out on the table. He could even smell the freshly baked pie, which was like heaven to him. Another afternoon tea. Was he being spoiled? Gran told him a few people were coming to welcome him home and, for a moment, he wondered if he was really back in England on leave and everything else was a dream.

Then a man came through the door, and it really sank in to Brian that he was 'dead'. He called out in surprise, 'Len!' Len was his father's younger cousin, who had passed over several years ago. Len welcomed him and they conversed by thought for a while as Brian was now beginning to get the hang of this telepathic kind of communication. Then Brian looked around and got a real shock.

His boyhood friend Bob was sitting on the other side of the table. Brian was overjoyed as Bob had died tragically in a boating accident when Brian was about eight years old and he had felt guilty all these years for not being able to save his friend. Bob explained his drowning was not Brian's fault, as it had been his time to pass over. He explained that sometimes we choose to have a short life so we can help others with lessons they need to learn in that lifetime. Brian was not really sure what he meant, but Bob told him all would become clear when he resumed his lessons later. It was only then that Brian suddenly realised that Bob was no longer a little boy. He appeared to be about the same age as Brian. Even so Brian was able to instantly recognise his old friend.

When I went back over this inter-life experience later, I was surprised that Bob had grown up in spirit, and yet Brian still knew him immediately. As usual M was able to help explain this phenomenon with a memory association. When I attended an old school reunion recently, it was great catching up with men I had not seen for many years. It was often really hard to put a name to a face but then, without warning, I started to get flashbacks of various schoolmates as they were all those years ago. I would only have to look at a face or sometimes a name tag and a much younger image would flash into my mind. A day or two later as I was working on this section of the book, it suddenly hit home. This is exactly the same process that allows us to recognise someone in the afterlife from a much earlier time. Thanks once again to my guide M!

Several other people then joined Brian for afternoon tea as his grandmother laughingly referred to it. He knew them all instantly, even though most of them were not part of his immediate past life. This was all very exciting, a bit like a surprise birthday party.

Then, a very attractive girl came in and stood at the back of the room, just quietly watching. Deep down Brian felt he knew her, but couldn't remember who she was. His grandmother read his thoughts and told him her name was Fleur. She was a member of his soul family and when he was fully recuperated she would accompany him back to join the rest of the family.

Brian was very surprised because he thought he was already with his soul family, but Gran explained he was currently in a kind of staging place—it was on a different level to the one that souls went to just after passing through the tunnel. When Brian looked back to where Fleur had been standing, she was gone. 'Don't worry, she'll be there when you're ready,' he was informed.

When everyone finally departed, Gran again led Brian to his room so he could rest. He was exhausted after all the excitement and even after going through the healing house, he was still in recovery mode. This wasn't surprising as the traumas of the trenches had left a deep imprint on his soul.

Brian's recuperation continued for what felt like several weeks. During this time he took long walks in the countryside, often visiting the seashore, as he regained his full strength. His grandmother was always there waiting for him when he got back to the village, which was very comforting. On these walks, Brian thought a lot about his welcome home party and the people he met up with after all those years. Later he realised he was no longer thinking of life on earth, but did not feel too guilty about it. It all seemed so far away. Eventually he was ready for the next stage of his journey to reconnect with his soul family. He was also impatient to see Fleur again.

20

God and the afterlife

*'I am ready to meet my Maker. Whether my Maker
is prepared for the great ordeal of meeting me is
another matter.'*
Sir Winston Churchill, 1874–1965

The traditional concept of God does not sit well with
everyone. We are so often led to believe in the image
of an old man with a long beard sitting on a giant throne.
We have been given the impression all too frequently of
an aloof being, seemingly devoid of love and emotion. But
there has not been one report from anyone in the afterlife, to
my knowledge, that has had contact with such an imposing
figure.

In a deep meditation I was given an image of God
that sits very comfortably with me. I was shown a large,
restless sea and was told this was an ocean of pure energy
representing the creative force of the cosmos. Part of this
energy has been used to create the souls that inhabit our

universe and beyond. We are all essentially part of the same source which we refer to as 'God' or 'the Creator'. So, it makes sense to me that we would desire to return to our original state—to go home—once we have finally achieved our purpose since separating from the source. This explains the biblical reference to people being made in the image of God, as an energetic image, rather than a physical one.

The tunnel travel experienced after bodily separation indicates a link, a kind of wormhole or portal between two worlds—the earth plane and the world of spirit. My understanding is the world of spirit is simply located in a different dimension of reality; that it actually occupies the same space we do but, as it vibrates at a vastly higher rate than life on earth, it is invisible to us. So, far from being separated from our loved ones who have passed over, they are really all around us—we just cannot see them using our normal vision. When they show themselves to us, they are actually slowing their vibration to match the third-dimensional density of our material world.

One theory suggests that our upper atmosphere, which we understand as gravity, is really part of the domain of spirit. If this is the case, then the planes of reality are layered on top of the earth, a bit like a giant onion. So, perhaps our gravity field forms part of the lower astral planes.

As I previously mentioned, Robert Monroe, a pioneer in out of body experiences, set up The Monroe Institute in the US to explore the astral realms.[1] Since Monroe's death, the institute has continued this work under the direction of 'Skip' Atwater.[2] Skip is a retired military officer who initially came to the institute while serving in the army, to officially set up a remote viewing unit for counter intelligence purposes. Remote viewing is the practice of leaving the body in astral form to experience other locations on earth, in the spirit world and on other planets.

The institute is open to the public, and also trains participants in out-of-body exploration. A friend and colleague, Jo Buchanan, who is a healer and author, did the course. She later told me how she was able to connect with souls after they had left their bodies and were relocating to the spirit world. Jo described one encounter she had with one young man, a friend of her daughter. This is her diary entry:

> Last night I was drifting in that state between conscious-
> ness and sleep, aware of being out of my body. Suddenly I
> was aware of a young man. I sensed his name was 'Rory'.
> I 'knew' that he had just committed suicide. Today, I felt
> strongly to ring my daughter back home. She was very
> upset about a friend of hers who had just committed
> suicide. His name was 'Gary'.

At first Jo had the impression of going down a tunnel at lightning speed with what she described as hundreds of bars of brightly coloured neon lights. The speed at which she was travelling made the bars of light turn into 'light snatches' which surrounded her.

The way Jo describes her tunnel experience is exactly the same vision I experience when connecting with the other side, or to my guides. I feel as if I am rushing down a wormhole with flashes of lights all around whizzing past me.

In his out-of-body experiences Monroe wrote about discarnate souls floating about as if seeking direction.[3] There are many mediums and other members of spiritualist groups who take it upon themselves to go into this space to help rescue these confused spirits and send them to the light. These same people also give their time and energies to earthbound spirits to help them cross over, as we saw earlier.

When these wandering souls clearly state they need assistance, spirit helpers always arrive to help them. But many discarnate spirits are still too attached to the earth plane, too caught up in their own thoughts and desires, to even see or trust the helpers from spirit. In my spiritual group one of our members, Tony, is a natural medium. In one session Tony went into a deep trance and connected with the spirit of a deceased woman from India. This woman's spirit was very distressed as she had been the victim of 'bride burning'. As a widow she had been doused with kerosene or petrol and set on fire, so she would be one less mouth to feed. Tony drew on the group energy to help this poor soul find her way into the light, and escape what she felt was an ignominious punishment for being a widow. So traumatised was this woman's soul she believed she would suffer torment for all time, simply because she had outlived her husband. This was a chilling experience, which had a deep impact on Tony. The other members of the group were also deeply affected. But once the spirit helpers came for the tortured woman's soul, we were all happy to have been a part of this rescue.

Part C
Adapting to Our New Conditions

21

Brian's new afterlife house

Eventually Brian's guide Markus came to collect Brian from his grandmother's house. Brian was becoming impatient about the next stage of his journey and he had begun to wonder about his soul family. When Markus appeared without warning beside Brian, he simply took hold of Brian's hand. It was the same sensation Brian felt when he left the battlefield in France on his way to the tunnel. The world around him started to fade. Then suddenly they were standing in a village by the sea.

Brian immediately recognised the scene: it was a painting he'd seen as a child—a typical Greek village with whitewashed houses and shops in narrow, winding lanes all leading down to a small beach flanked by stone walls. Several fishing boats were tied to the walls, and fishing nets were stretched out on the sand while they were being repaired.

Brian felt like a child who had been given the perfect Christmas present and he looked at Markus in amazement.

'You always wanted to live in a Greek seaside town,' Markus said, 'so now you can.'

'How on earth did I get here?' Brian asked his guide.

Markus smiled broadly and replied, 'To start with, you are not on earth.' Then he explained, 'You created this village yourself.'

'Did I? How?'

Markus told Brian how in the afterlife we can create everything we wish for with our thoughts and memories. The Greek village was so strong in Brian's memory that he automatically manifested it. Markus told him that if he didn't want to live here, he could move, simply by creating a new place to live with his thoughts.

After the horrors of war-torn France and Belgium, this village was indeed paradise to Brian. As he looked out at the clear, shining water he was reminded that here there was no mud, no rats and lice, and no fear of being blown apart by the enemy. The temperature was warm and the sky was the kind of blue he had not seen before in England, Belgium or France. Above all, it was so quiet and peaceful.

'No, no, I am very happy to live here,' Brian reassured Markus. 'Do I have to rent a house?'

Markus told Brian that a house was already waiting for him, and that there was no rent to pay as there is no money in the spirit world. Brian was very puzzled at this. Markus told him that as he had been through a lot of pain in the war, memories of the afterlife would come back to him gradually. In the meantime all he had to do was to settle into his new surroundings.

As Brian looked around, he was surprised to see a small two-storey house near the waterfront. It appeared to be the same house as the one in the painting he had loved as a child. Markus simply nodded, indicating this house was his, and Brian, now confused and shocked, just grinned.

The house had seemed small from the outside, but once inside Brian was very surprised to find it was spacious. Strangely, it was also very similar to his childhood home in Devon, and even the furniture was the same. Markus explained that Brian had created the Greek village scene based on a painting in his memory. Having no idea what a Greek house looked like on the inside, Brian's imagination had created an interior based on his own limited experience.

The guide looked at his charge with the love of a father for his child. 'You can create whatever you want,' he said. 'You can even make the house bigger or smaller. If you want to change something just think about it until it happens.'

Brian thought he was getting the hang of it now and remarked, cheekily, that he loved the house but it was rather sparsely furnished. Markus, pleased to see Brian enjoying himself, told him to form a picture in his mind of the kind of furnishings he would like. Brian immediately thought of two very comfortable armchairs—and like magic they appeared. Without hesitation, Brian flopped into one with a big sigh.

22
Life review

The afterlife is, as we discovered earlier, made up of many levels of existence and we go to the level our spirit has achieved. Once we have gone through the healing centre, we do eventually return to our soul family, but there are a few stages in between.

In case you are thinking we do not have to account for our actions in our last life when we return to our spiritual home—think again! Forget all that stuff about judgement day and the wrath of God. We go to see the Council of Elders instead.

According to M, the Council of Elders is a group of highly evolved spiritual beings who exist to inspire and help us on our soul's journey. (The Elders are explained in chapter 25.) When we meet the Council they take us lovingly through our last life in minute detail, examining every thought and every action. It is very much like the instant replay we see in TV sporting events and, from all accounts, it takes very little time. It may be a rush of information through our mind, or seen in our mind's eye; either way, our life is played out around us, complete in every detail. It's an important stage in the progression of each soul.

During our life review we are able to look at every experience we had in our life: the positive sides, as well as the mistakes we made. Most importantly, during the course of this review we are also able to graphically experience how our actions affected others. We come to realise that so often the small details were what were most important. It may merely have been a thoughtful act or a random act of kindness, and while they were not necessarily our finest moments—from our limited perspective—they were usually the times we showed unconditional love. We come to see that these were the gestures that mattered, because they were loving in nature. Love is the key word here, as this is the driving force of the universe.

On many occasions we come to realise that what we thought were disastrous mistakes turned out to be great learning experiences for ourselves and other people. As in an intricate drama, our life's complicated plot often has many unexpected twists and turns. Fortunately it all unfolds by the final curtain.

The Elders don't sit there condemning our mistakes with the intention of making us feel guilty. Rather it is us as individuals who closely analyse what has happened. We realise where we succeeded and where we disappointed ourselves and others. By now the veil which descends at the beginning of each earthly lifetime has been lifted. We are now able to fully remember what our purpose and ambitions for that life were. If indeed there is any judging to be done, we do it ourselves, in a positive way.

Our guide usually comes with us as we visit the Elders. This is usually the same guide who worked with us before we reincarnated, helping us before that incarnation to work out the karmic goals and ambitions that we wanted to achieve in our next life.

Guides are tolerant and understanding and never judgmental, as they too have experienced many lives and fully understand the pressures, successes and disappointments during each lifetime. Our guide works with us acting as a spiritual mentor, helping us understand and come to terms with what we have made of our life.

23

The Akashic Records

During the period in between lives we also have access to the Akashic Records. These records hold all the details of every life we have ever lived on earth, as well as elsewhere. Periodic study in between incarnations helps us to understand our past directions, and to know what we need to aim for in our next lifetime. Access to the Akashic Records, also known as the Hall of Records, is available to those of us who reach a certain level in the afterlife, as part of our studies in between lives. The knowledge we gain there is then blotted out when we are reborn. At the beginning of each life a veil comes down between us and the spirit world, as it would be far too confusing during each lifetime to have knowledge of all our past lives as well. As mentioned before, it's what's happening for us now which is paramount. To live in the past is pointless.

A few psychics are able to access the Akashic Records and help people understand more of their life purpose.

Edgar Cayce stated that the Akashic Records contain every deed, word, feeling, thought and intent that has ever occurred at any time in the history of the world. While there may be only a handful of people on earth at any one time able to access these records, others have developed their own special methods.

The Naadi Palm Leaf readers, for example, are famous in India for having produced some amazing insights into people's life stories from their readings. With only a birth date, a name and the gender requested, these amazing readers help people discover themselves and their life's purpose. They also provide details of appropriate karmic past lives, as well as names and detailed particulars of family members and other people affecting their lives.

The palm leaves are described as fairly compact and covered in miniscule writing on both sides. They are copied exactly whenever a leaf perishes. Allegedly written in Sanskrit and Tamil more than 5000 years ago by Lord Shiva, and compiled by various sages, the details contained on each leaf are very precise. It was prophesised that certain people will one day access their leaf and that this information is waiting for the seeker at the ordained time. Certain leaves also contain predictions of world events. The recent global economic collapse had been written in the leaves long ago, along with great climate changes forecast to be triggered by the sun in 2009 and then in late 2012 to early 2013. Each leaf is different and the leaf reader has to find our particular one from a repository of literally tens of thousands of leaves.

British medium Angela Donovan and her husband, Andrew, consulted the leaf readers and were given information which could only have come from the spirit realm. Before he encountered the Naadi Palm Leaf readers Andrew was a sceptic. But during the reading he was told his mother and father's names, that his father was in the armed forces and many other personal details which 'staggered' him. The reader identified Andrew's university degree and at what age he gave up his profession to become a writer. Andrew was also given details of his attempts to adopt a child. He told me his stomach was heaving after finding his life story had been set down on a leaf written thousands of years ago.

The leaf reader told Andrew his mother was very ill back home in England, and Andrew was shaken when asked if he had an undertaker in mind. When he returned to his hotel, still dazed, the receptionist hurried up to Andrew asking him to ring England urgently. Much to his amazement he was then told his mother was gravely ill and not expected to live. The reader also spoke of the sins of Andrew's past lives, which he had to resolve in this lifetime. He was able to readily identify with these aspects of his character, albeit reluctantly. Andrew's ideas about spirituality and pre-ordained events were changed that day in India.

I had a personal reading with a visiting Indian astrologer who was allegedly able to read the Akashic Records. He, too, used small palm leaves and produced some amazing insights about my two marriages. He identified dates for both weddings and subsequent divorces, along with very accurate details of both partners, as well as my children. He told me my marriages were the completion of karma between the parties, and that I was now free to pursue my spiritual path. He told me I would become completely spiritual several years after my second marriage ended, which has virtually happened. Not everything has turned out exactly as he stated. There were other predictions that have not yet come to pass, but time will tell. Of course, as with every reading, there is also the aspect of free will. We each make choices which alter our destiny.

The Akashic Records have been spoken and written about by many past civilisations, and it would appear as though a fair portion of our life's path is truly written in stone. The logical mind asks if perhaps we are merely puppets—for although we set out to achieve certain goals each lifetime, if all is decided in advance then where is the free will in that?

I think our life's journey is more like a self-correcting computer program. When we make certain decisions a train of events is triggered, and the records adjust accordingly. This theme was explored in the film *Sliding Doors* where two totally different scenarios were played out. Gwyneth Paltrow's character catches a train in the first plotline, but just misses it in the second. Her life then takes two different directions before it melds into a finale which takes both possibilities into account.

This approach may be truer than we realise. Quantum research indicates there is no past, present and future, but that we are actually living all our lives at the same time. Linear time does not exist. I find this a very hard concept to get my head around, but maybe it would help explain the Naadi Palm Leaf readers.

24

How karma affects us

Shortly after Brian settled into his new premises, Markus arrived unexpectedly and beckoned him to follow. They soon arrived at the entrance to a very large, imposing building with an extremely high pitched roof. They went up the stairs and into a huge reception area, which seemed to go on and on forever. There was no receptionist on duty to give any directions, however Brian intuitively knew where to go and soon found himself entering a small private alcove dominated by a large leather chair.

Markus told him to sit down and close his eyes. Almost immediately various images and related messages began to flow into Brian's mind. He watched as a parade of faces rushed by and recognised some of them from his immediate past life. He was told the others were from some of his previous lives. Even though it seemed to be over in an instant, the volume of information was intense.

As Brian tried to make sense of it all, Markus explained the purpose of Brian's short lifetime was to understand the meaning of sacrifice, as well as the stupidity and futility of war. Having just served on the Western Front Brian needed no convincing. During this life review he discovered that he had been involved in many wars during previous lifetimes. Whereas in past lives Brian had led men into battle who in turn were killed, this time he had to experience dying because of someone else's commands. As karma basically means achieving balance, in his last life Brian had to explore what it was like to have his power, along with his very existence, taken away.

As Brian reflected on his past lives, Markus pointed out that Brian had experienced a number of lives as a soldier. Conversely Brian had also been a member of the priesthood in various civilisations and religions. Markus then explained that everyone has to do this past-life review work before meeting with the Council of Elders. Each of us is required to put our past into perspective, so we can understand what these wise souls wish for us to learn about ourselves.

As Brian focused once more on the life he had just completed, it was time to explore more fully its impact on others. Markus then gently reminded Brian that his son, Simon, would grow up never knowing his father. That was to be the karma this soul chose to experience. Markus added that Brian's wife, Jenny, was so shattered by his death that she, too, would pass over soon. This meant young Simon would be raised by family members.

Brian's was a short life in terms of earth time, less than 20 years, but the ongoing effects could not be ignored. Brian came to see his marriage as a very brief relationship between two immature young people, but he felt remorse at not being able to be there in Jenny's time of need. He was then shown images of young Simon growing up to become a very influential and wealthy businessman. It was a very emotional occasion and Brian felt very sad he would not be part of his son's life as he grew. He determined to return to earth as soon as he was permitted, to see how his family was coping in those dire times.

As they left the building, Markus confirmed Brian would soon appear before the Council of Elders for his assessment, before at last being able to rejoin his soul family. After that he would be able to visit his earth family too. Brian, still reeling from the entire experience, had no idea he was to experience a much deeper, more direct understanding of his warlike past when he met with the Council of Elders.

My guide in this life, M, broke into my thoughts at this point saying that Jenny has returned in my current life as one of my family, so we could be together in some way. All he would tell me is that she is one of my three granddaughters.

25

Meeting the Council of Elders

*'Reincarnation is neither absurd nor useless . . . it is no
more surprising to be born twice than to be born once . . .
everything in nature is resurrection.'*
VOLTAIRE, 1694–1798

Apart from the re-education process of the healing
and life review on the lower astral plane, the only
other ordeal facing the deceased soul is our meeting with
the Council of Elders.

The Elders know us from the depth of our soul, literally
from every level of our incarnation.

All accounts of the Elders describe them as compassionate and supportive, a gentle group of people who
lovingly encourage each soul to examine the life just led.
Instead of criticism and stern words, they encourage self-
forgiveness, and further learning and development, before
embarking on the next life. Judgement by others does not

exist in the afterlife; however, although the Elders do not judge, the soul involved in the life review is often their own harshest critic.

Mistakes made during our life are explained by the wise Elders as opportunities for learning. The hardest lesson to bear is to see how our actions have affected and hurt others. Sometimes we are made to 'feel' or experience that hurt, so we, too, can understand the impact and consequences of our actions. But we are never condemned or cast away by the spirit world.

The Council of Elders also decides on how far our soul has evolved after each life—whether we have earned the right to advance to a higher level, or have to reincarnate to keep learning. When it is time to reincarnate, they also advise souls on the best direction for the next life.

The Elders are very advanced spiritual beings. They have attained enlightenment after many lives on earth as well as in other worlds. Some reports say that they have never incarnated, but my experience revealed otherwise. The Elders understand the mistakes we make and do their best to help us in our soul's journey. There are many such groups of Elders in the world of spirit. They gently inspire souls to spend the inter-life sojourn in positive ways to prepare for the next reincarnation.

It would seem logical that unless these Elders had experienced life on earth themselves, they could not be completely empathetic. However, human logic is not always a reliable guide in the afterlife.

Some reports describe the Elders as old men in long white flowing gowns. They are usually depicted with white hair and beards, though some also tell of those who are bald. It seems that once again we are able to create stereotypes to satisfy our own ideas of what a group of wise beings would look like. It makes sense that these Councils would also comprise wise women, as the world of spirit embraces oneness in all aspects of life.

Nancy Canning, a past-life and inter-life therapist, takes people into their between-life experiences through hypnotic regression. She describes the Elders as being very wise spiritual beings and confirms they have ceased reincarnating on earth. She has found there is no set number of Elders who work with us. In her experience there can be anywhere from three to 12 in each session.

There is not just one set of Elders. Everyone has their own allocated group working with them. While these beings hold us accountable, they don't judge. There is deep love and patience and they are with us to help us grow. Nancy describes the support of the Elders as pure unconditional love. Interestingly, the same group of Elders do not stay with us all the time. It depends on where we are going as well as the stage to which our soul has reached.

Our guide normally accompanies us into the chamber to meet the Elders, but stands back respectfully to one side to allow free communication. Our guides are also there to help us with any communication problems.

When Markus accompanied Brian to meet the Elders they went up a wide set of steps leading to a classical Greek-style building. For some reason Brian imagined entering a dark, wooded, old-fashioned 'courtroom' with a bewigged judge peering over his spectacles as the perpetrator was bundled into the dock. Perhaps Brian had read about this scenario in a book, or perhaps it had happened in another life. At this point he experienced flashes of a past life where he was hanged for being a thief, so it must still have been on his conscience!

In stark contrast to what he expected, Brian found himself in what seemed to be a very bright, spacious area. Far from being judged or feeling as if he was on trial, he felt a lightness of being and a lot of supportive energy surrounding him. The Elders did not sit at a table or on a raised platform, but seemed to float around him, not needing to sit or stand. Brian saw that each of the Elders was surrounded by a radiant light, which gave the impression they were wearing long robes.

Standing with them all positioned around him, Brian felt as if he was waiting for some kind of assessment, almost as if it was a job interview. But there was no sense of tension in the meeting, simply a wonderful feeling of love and support.

The Council informed Brian that before he was born he had agreed to live a short life and had accepted the inevitability of an early death. They reinforced the message given to him earlier by Markus, that the main purpose of Brian's recent life was to fully realise the futility of war. They knew Markus had already told him about several previous lives as a warrior, when he had taken many lives. Now they wanted to show Brian some graphic images of these acts of violence.

Brian was shown several visions. In the first visit Brian relived his life as one of a group of warriors on horseback, sweeping across open country and attacking villages, killing, raping, looting and burning. The perspective then changed, and he experienced the terror and pain of one of the women that he had assaulted and put to the sword. The pain and anguish of this woman was palpable. He was able to experience and feel it for himself, which was very frightening to him.

In another life he was a Roman soldier, who ended up being murdered for the callous way he treated the local women. These visions were far more disturbing than his session with Markus and Brian felt very distressed at his actions. As he struggled to take everything in, he realised he had some pretty hard lessons to learn about war.

Then the Council reviewed his last life. Although he had been forced to defend himself whilst fighting in the trenches in France, Brian had come to a realisation about the futility and brutality of war long before he was killed. Being a soldier and taking lives was a very troubling and upsetting experience for him and he wanted none of it. This was despite him making the choice to join the army in the first place.

Once that realisation came flooding back into his conscious mind, the Elders appeared very satisfied that Brian had indeed discovered at long last the pointlessness of war. They informed him he would not be placed in a position of killing or taking part in battle again. Another way of expressing this experience was that Brian had completed his karma as a warrior, and could now evolve to other experiences.

The Elders also showed Brian visions of other lifetimes as a priest and shaman at various times in history, including the Egyptian and Mayan times. Brian got the distinct impression this was a theme the Elders wished him to further explore in the future. They told Brian he would find out more details about this aspect of his previous life before taking on his next life. Far from feeling guilty or even admonished, Brian felt a surge of love from these wonderful beings.

•

Brian's Council of Elders comprised five ascended beings. I later discovered if someone has had a short life as he did, the number is usually fairly low; a long life with many directions and experiences to examine could attract a larger assembly. As an observer I did not see or feel that there were any familiar faces in the group, but I kept getting the name Gladstone all through my regression. The only Gladstone that was remotely familiar to me was the name of the former prime minister of England. Brian would have probably learned about Gladstone at school, and M later confirmed that this was indeed the same person.

It turns out William Gladstone died in 1898 after four terms as British prime minister, when Brian would only have been about two years of age. M told me Gladstone was a very advanced soul and was now sitting as a new member on the Council of Elders. I suppose as Brian was growing up, the name of Gladstone would still have been mentioned a lot at home and at school, even in a small village in Devon, so it's no surprise the name jumped out so clearly. It turned out that Brian's father was a great follower of Gladstone, who was a staunch supporter of the Church of England. His father apparently also shared many of Gladstone's beliefs, according to M.

William Gladstone is still regarded, alongside Winston Churchill, as one of the finest prime ministers ever to lead government in Britain. Not only an astute politician, he had a strong humanitarian side as well. In 1840 when Gladstone decided to rescue and rehabilitate London's prostitutes, he set out walking the streets of the city himself, encouraging the women he encountered to change their ways. Gladstone continued this practice for decades, even after he was elected prime minister. He was generally known as a very decent and moral person with high religious principles.

For some strange reason I have felt compelled to mention William Gladstone here, even though I have no conscious interest in or link to him.[1] M informs me he will be in the Council of Elders I will face at the end of this life. That would also explain to me why he came through so strongly in my regression. (So I had better stay in his good books!)

We must all face a similar Council meeting when we pass over, so there is no need for fear or concern. The Elders help us realise where we succeeded and where we missed out. The mistakes we have made will not prevent the growth of our soul, if we learn from them and progress. People are often surprised that small random acts of kindness are praised by the Elders, whereas contrived acts such as charity donations or pre-meditated acts of goodwill go unmentioned. We may believe we have acted in a generous and thoughtful manner during our life, but the Elders see further than we do.

This first meeting with the Elders is to help us understand what we have or have not achieved for the growth of our soul. The Elders also usually provide guidance on how to ascend to the higher realms. If the decision involves reincarnation on earth they let us know that our next meeting will concern the choice for our next life.

Bob Olson wrote a very insightful article about being regressed into the afterlife by Nancy Canning.[2] In it, he recalls being taken to the Council of Elders soon after he passed from his last life in 1643. He spoke of seven beings of light, high-level spiritual masters, who sat around an oval table with him. He saw them not as men or women, but as masses of light. He was able to still sense their personalities, and felt that they had body-like movements. He recalled that the most overwhelming feeling he received was that they loved him deeply. He described their love as being 'so intense that I burst into tears' the moment he first encountered them.

Once in front of the Council of Elders, he immediately realised they were not there to judge him for the mistakes he had made in his past life as a man named George. In fact, he felt their great compassion because he was harshly judging his previous actions himself. As he faced the Elders he experienced a 'past-life recall', going through his previous life all over again, but with a much greater understanding of the successes and failures he had made in that life as George.

Bob Olson had a second regression session with Nancy Canning some time later, where he once again met the Council of Elders. This time he was able to ask them questions about his current life, receiving some very pertinent and useful advice.

From this we can deduce that the Elders monitor our lives whether we are in spirit or in the physical world and that it is their place to help us evolve in any way possible. Nancy recommends clients bring a list of questions for the Elders when she works with them, as she is able to put people directly in touch with their Elders to gain insights for their current life.

There is nothing strange or unusual about the concept of a council of wise elders. History teaches us that many different civilisations through the ages have been guided and even ruled by a group of wise beings. Once again it is obvious that the concept of 'as above, so below' applies, as we can choose to honour the principle of wisdom and experience.

It is only in recent years that the wisdom and experience of our elders is being ignored in our world, one obsessed with youth and beauty. Perhaps this too will change in time and wisdom gained by experience will be once again respected.

26

Soul families
and soul mates

Soul families are close-knit groups that stay together throughout the ages. They work together, encouraging and supporting each member of the family in their efforts for spiritual growth. When souls are reunited after each lifetime there is a great feeling of joy and sometimes relief at being together again. It is the ultimate support group with unconditional love being the binding force.

We relate to members of our soul family in much the same way as all families in life do, except in the afterlife there is an extremely deep connection. We may play various roles when we live our lives on earth, or other worlds for that matter, but we create every experience out of pure love for the other members of our group, so we may all learn and grow together.

The size of our particular family varies, just as in earthly life. One thing we can be sure of is that we immediately recognise each member of our family, even though there may have been no direct contact with them in the previous life. Many people are overjoyed, and some very surprised, to be reunited with souls they have known for a very long time.

Of course, not all members of the family are there in the afterlife at the same time. Certain souls could well be experiencing an earthly incarnation at that time. So it is very much like going to a wedding or a funeral and seeing members of your family that have been scattered around the world, but have come together briefly. Some you see regularly, some not for a while. Others you have not caught up with for a long time. And then there are those unable to be there because of health problems, work commitments, etc.

We do not incarnate with our full spirit energy, which may surprise a lot of people. We are able to choose how much of our energy we wish to take into each life. This means there is always a small but significant part of ourselves remaining in the spirit world. This is often referred to as 'the higher self'. So when we are reunited with our soul family, there will be those who are there in full energy, while some will be there at a much lower energetic level. However, in effect, we do reconnect with the entire group.

The higher self that remains behind in the spirit world is in contact with our master guide and/or guardian angel.

The higher self could be described as our inner source of guidance in life. This, of course, is not our only source of guidance. During each incarnation we may have more than one guide. Some guides come and go at various times in our life, as we grow and change. In my current life, M is the latest in a series of guides who have joined me for specific periods of time. Guides have certain strengths and abilities. As we develop spiritually we can draw new guides to us. They change much like school teachers. A new guide will often come to us when we are going through some kind of transformation in our lives.

•

Brian was talking to Markus, sitting in the very comfortable lounge room of his Mediterranean seaside cottage. He was just about to ask about the members of his soul family when there was a knock on the door and a tall man, who appeared to be in his early thirties, entered. Brian intuitively recognised this man as a member of his soul family. While Brian could not remember his name, the man looked very familiar, and deep down Brian knew they had shared many experiences together and there was a lot of love between them.

Without saying a word the man created a chair for himself and sat quietly next to Markus. They both proceeded to show Brian some images from his past-life experiences. One life saw this new man and Brian fighting together as Roman soldiers, in another life they were Franciscan monks. Brian's head started to spin trying to take it all in. Although this man was not part of his immediate past life, Markus told Brian they would be reunited in his next life, *my* current life. 'All this will be explained later,' Markus said when he saw Brian's look of confusion.

'My next life!' Brian said. 'I've only just finished one, and you're already talking about another one.'

Several other people then came into the house and, in some strange way, Brian knew them all, even though he did not remember them from his last life. It was like going away for a long time, coming home and seeing friends and family you had not seen for many years. It was at the same time strange and wonderfully exciting.

Brian found out later they all lived nearby, and that they would see a lot of each other from then on. They were not members of his immediate soul family, but were from neighbouring soul groups. When he asked why they were all living in a Greek village, Markus explained with a smile that each soul creates their own reality. While Brian saw his surroundings as a Mediterranean fishing village, they saw and experienced what they had created for themselves. Brian made a mental note to ask them next time he saw them where they were living.

Markus also informed Brian that the first man who came to visit was preparing to return to earth, but that his life was not going to be a long one. The Elders had decided Brian and he would have another life together and that this person would be his son. Brian then recalled that this man, who he had fought alongside as a Roman soldier and lived with as a fellow monk, was the one who had come to see him when he first crossed over. He was there having tea with Brian's grandmother. Yet it all seemed so long ago, so much had happened since then.

Reading Brian's confused thoughts, Markus suggested they leave so Brian could think things over and start his new life quietly. The guide suggested Brian take time to explore his new surroundings in the Greek village, as he would meet all kinds of interesting people there. Little did Brian realise how true these words would turn out to be.

•

In my next session with M, I watched on fascinated as Brian had another unexpected visitor. It was someone he had been longing to catch up with for some time and he was lost for words when Fleur suddenly appeared at his door.

As an observer I was able to look at Fleur closely for the first time, and recognised her energy immediately, even though the way she looked was not familiar to me.

My guide M interrupted my reverie, communicating only one word, 'Carol'.

My immediate thought was of my second wife in this current lifetime. Though we have been divorced for more than 20 years, the memories came flooding back. Carol and I met and came together in a very mysterious and romantic way in Greece and Egypt. After a storybook beginning we went on to have an exciting but tumultuous marriage. The karmic nature of this relationship made immediate sense to me. I assumed she would be a member of my soul family.

It just proves how wrong you can be by jumping to conclusions!

'Not that Carol,' M said, almost impatiently, 'the other Carol. Think back to earlier in your current life.'

When it hit me who he meant I was absolutely stunned. Another look at Fleur confirmed who Carol from this current life was. Suddenly I was no longer in the Greek village, but back in the 21st century. I was still in very deep meditation, but needed to take in what I had just experienced. It is a strange procedure and difficult to explain. On one hand I am an observer, watching events unfold for Brian during his afterlife; on the other hand, I can 'become' Brian and empathise with the situation he's facing. It's like being split into two different parts which are working together.[1]

So what of Carol and Fleur?

I had trained in the theatre as a young man before going into broadcasting. At drama school Carol and I were always cast as the lovers in plays like *The Importance of Being Earnest*, *Hamlet*, *The Tempest*, and, you guessed it, *Romeo and Juliet*. It was hardly surprising that we also became close friends, and Carol was my date at my 21st birthday party. She was also my first love.

A few months after we finished drama school, I was appointed as an announcer with a major network and I was posted to a TV station in another state, so we went our separate ways. My mother was most upset as she adored Carol and had hoped we would marry one day. Several years later I was back in my home city, working on commercial radio. Carol came in to the studios to be interviewed, as she was starring in a new play. We instantly reconnected and with my first marriage going through a rocky period, we began a love affair. However, like Romeo and Juliet, we were 'star crossed lovers', and our all-too-brief relationship ended disastrously. Despite searching for her, I have never seen Carol again to this day, but have always felt devastated over what happened. Emotions ranging from unfulfilled love to guilt remain with me, even now.

When I found out Carol and I were part of the same soul family, it answered many of my questions. M later told me that we had agreed to meet briefly in my current life, to help each other learn some vital lessons. Just what those lessons are I have still not completely discovered.

•

We can't discuss soul families without also discussing soul mates. The concept is an appealing one, and has been taken up by romance writers for many years, while Hollywood has turned the whole thing into a soap opera. There are many people who believe they will never find true happiness until they meet their soul mate. However, the truth is we may have several soul mates in our earthly life, or even none at all. A member of your soul family is naturally a soul mate, because you share many characteristics at a soul level. They may reincarnate at the same time as yourself and may be your sibling, a partner, a close friend or even someone you feel is your enemy.

American author and hypnotherapist Michael Newton, maintains that it is not very common for our parents to be part of our soul family.[2] This at first might seem strange, but as we are separated in life by generation gaps, it would explain in part why we come from different soul groups. Perhaps this difference also offers more opportunities for soul growth. Having regressed large numbers of people in intense regression programs, Newton describes soul families as small clusters whose members are closely united for all eternity.

So, how did these soul groups form in the first place and under whose direction? And does a soul group only advance to new spheres once all its members have reached the same level?

When I put this to my guide M, he explained that all soul families were originally created by 'higher beings' far above the level of the Elders. Though there are exceptions, he also confirmed souls normally advance as a group, which represents the true spirit of team work. Small soul clusters link with neighbouring soul groups that are closely aligned, and they all interact with each other as they grow individually and as a group. The various members of these soul clusters that join forces often form close relationships in their ongoing incarnations. This is why we can feel drawn to certain people in life, often despite emotional and physical differences.

Though people may be from the same soul family, it does not necessarily mean that they are to be 'together' in their life on earth. Many members of soul families never even come into contact with each other on earth. They may be living in different parts of the world, or simply choosing very different life experiences. These separate experiences will obviously be something special to share once they are reunited in the non-physical world.

When it is time to start planning our next incarnation, members of our soul family will often agree to play different roles to help each other to learn and grow. Not all interactions will be happy or easy, as earthly life is about soul growth. More on this later, when we get to future life planning.

27

Exploring the village

Wanting to learn more about his Greek afterlife village, Brian asked Markus to accompany him on an exploratory tour, so he could see what lay beyond his spirit house in this idyllic place. Markus agreed to guide Brian, from a distance.

Brian began to wander around the seaside village, exploring the back lanes and enjoying discovering the local buildings. As he took it all in, he realised it was so foreign to his life back in England, with its stone-paved streets and twisty alleyways. He was having a lovely time, until something struck him out of the blue. There were all these quaint whitewashed houses, rows of shops and taverns in this picturesque town, but where were the people?

Markus had told him he would meet all kinds of interesting people here, but to Brian's amazement he soon discovered his village was completely deserted, except for him—the lone wanderer.

Markus explained that as Brian had created this place from his thoughts, if he also wanted people there, he had to invite them in to be part of his world. This made sense to Brian. He had been shown how to create his own house in its own setting, but that was all he visualised. It was almost like a large film set or theatre waiting for the cast and crew to arrive to make it come alive.

As I observed Brian from my present-day perspective this realisation hit home: in life, everything we create or attract starts with a thought; every action, every reaction, has consequences. The same is true of the afterlife. For example, we may want more love in our life, or a more fulfilling job, but without working on it, it may never happen. Once again, the principle of 'As above, so below' applied to Brian's situation. How often do we retreat from the world around us, taking refuge in our house or room, to recover from the stresses of the day? We create a cave to shut out all the nasties. At the same time we can isolate ourselves from the world.

The temptation was for Brian to instantly create a bunch of neighbours to 'magic up' a ready-made village, but Markus suggested Brian step out of his comfort zone to see what lay beyond. He showed Brian through a gateway that Brian hadn't previously noticed, and instantly they found themselves in the middle of a busy town centre. People were going about their daily business and the place was teeming with life. As it turned out many others had also created this same village as their spirit home, though the way they saw and experienced it was through their own unique vision.

All this was happening at the edge of Brian's new home. So, he didn't have to create neighbours, they were already there! All he had to do was join in with them. The wonderful thing was that when he needed to escape the crowd, his little Greek house was just a thought away.

Once Brian 'tuned in' to the other people, the village came to life. There were villagers in the street and some waved and called out '*Yassou*' which Markus explained was a Greek greeting. Once again it hit home to me as I watched Brian how we create our physical world from our thoughts, and how important it is to be aware of their power.

Markus told Brian that he would have no trouble communicating with his neighbours as he had experienced a past life in a similar village many lifetimes ago. That explained why he felt completely at home there. Marcus also explained language was no barrier in the spirit world, as we all communicate with our thoughts in spirit, which then become a universal language.

Brian soon discovered he could also invite people to visit or even to stay if he wished. He knew his mother would love the village, and determined to get her there as soon as she was able to leave the healing centre. Suddenly

Fleur popped into his mind and as if he had the power of magic to summon her, she walked through the door. She had been reading Brian's thoughts and had been waiting for the invitation to visit. No need for telephones or letters in the afterlife, he mused. They went into the living room and had a wonderful telepathic chat.

The whole concept of thought-language is hard to explain in earth terms, but it is entirely natural in the afterlife. Fleur told Brian that they were indeed part of the same soul family, and that they also have had a lovely sibling-like relationship in spirit. Although they had shared many lives and would be together again, they were not meant to have a marriage-like relationship on earth. After she left, Brian realised the pure love they shared and looked forward to seeing a lot more of her.

When I came out of this particular meditation I realised that my spiritual relationship with Fleur explained what had happened earlier in my current life, and why Carol and I have now lost contact. We each achieved what was needed in this lifetime for us to grow. We are very closely linked and I look forward to our eventual reunion in our soul family.

28

Brian meets
his soul group

'The miracle is this—the more we share, the more we have.'
MR SPOCK (LEONARD NIMOY) IN *Star Trek*

When Markus came to Brian's house to inform him it was time to reconnect with his soul group, Brian was very excited, but a touch apprehensive. He had already started getting flashes of past activities with the group, nothing concrete, but he was not sure now what to expect.

Once again he held Markus's hand and they were instantly transported to a spectacular pyramid-shaped building which seemed to be constructed of pure transparent light. It appeared to be floating in the air but was anchored at each corner of the base by different beams of light. The building was breathtakingly beautiful, and Brian paused to admire it before they went inside.

On entering, Brian suddenly found himself in an open space. He looked around and saw there were several other people there, who he intuitively recognised immediately, as they warmly welcomed him back into their midst. There were five other members of his soul group present, and each was accompanied by their guide. Brian was very happy to see Fleur there. I was most interested to hear them refer to Brian by his spirit name, Voxon, and a few even shortened it to Vox.

Although this was the first time they had all met since Brian's passing, strangely enough he felt no rush of emotions which often happens when loved ones are reunited after a long absence. Markus explained that was because we keep in touch with our soul group at night during our dreams. This is when our astral body separates from our physical body, and it regularly returns to its spirit home during this time, for regeneration and for ongoing education by spending time with its guide. Many of these sessions held during sleep allow for getting together with our soul group, some of whom are living in spirit, while others are also visiting in astral form. Also, as we have discussed earlier, even when we reincarnate, a part of our energy always remains with our soul group. So in essence we are never really apart.

Brian was given pride of place in the group circle. He felt exhilarated at being with these special people again. There's a very strong sense of belonging in soul groups, based on pure acceptance, support and unconditional love. For Brian it felt like coming home.

Once Brian settled in, his soul group started discussing warfare associated with their various life experiences, and its ramifications. As the discussion became more involved, Brian noticed they were surrounded by a series of visuals of historic battle scenes in which they had been involved in past lives. Their guides confirmed they had all been involved in war in at least one incarnation.

Markus reminded Brian they are also able to access past lives when they meet in the Hall of Records, where the Akashic Records—the complete history of every action and thought we have ever had—are stored. Only special meetings were conducted here, and they only had to think of the past to be surrounded by the relevant visions.

As their discussion progressed, Brian saw graphic scenes swirling around of himself as a warrior in many past lives, including Greek and Roman times as well as in more modern settings. He also watched on as a couple of his soul family members took part in the fighting during the French Revolution. Even though they were street fighters and not soldiers at this time, the principle was the same. Brian then remembered the words of the Council of Elders reminding him that he had now completed this human experience. This gave him a great sense of comfort and relief while reliving some of the brutal actions of the past.

Curious to know more, Brian asked about the other lives he had led, apart from those when he was involved in war. Markus simply smiled, explaining Brian had many experiences in past lifetimes which would be re-examined later. He went on to say that we all comprise several different layers of energy, and as he spoke Brian started to experience a strange sensation. It was almost like some aspects of himself were being pulled together inside him. Markus told him he was fully merging with the soul energy he had left behind in spirit.

The soul group session continued with a lot of lively discussion. Then, suddenly, they were joined by a young man in astral form. I got a real surprise and was jerked out of my regression as Brian back to the present day as I recognised this young man as my oldest friend in this lifetime, Roger Cook. Roger and I had met at university and then worked at the same broadcasting network. Though he later went to live in England and became a household name on TV there, we have stayed close over the years. While we may not see each other often, when we do catch up, we just automatically take up where we left off. Though he is now semi-retired, Roger appeared in the group looking young and fit and around 30 years old.

Interestingly we have inspired each other in this lifetime, and Roger has always felt more like a brother to me. I guess seeing him in my regressed state was hardly surprising under the circumstances, but it startled me nevertheless. Roger's former self said he was fighting in a desert war and needed the group's support. After he left, Markus told the group he would soon be joining them in full spirit.

As I write it still gives me an eerie feeling as I observe my own spirit energy and its afterlife activities, connecting with people in my current life. This is a wonderful example of life where the quantum aspect of past, present and future may well be all happening at the same time.

29
Paradise found

The afterlife Plane of Illusion is not referred to as 'paradise' for nothing. For starters the weather is sublime. The temperature is neither too hot nor too cold but 'just right', and soft light bathes the whole world constantly, despite the fact that there is no sun in the sky. There is no night and day because there is no sun, and time as we know it does not exist. People are able to indulge in many activities without the need for sleep. However, if you feel the urge you can close your eyes for a while, and awake feeling completely refreshed.

You also choose what kind of clothes you wish to wear. Many people opt for a simple kind of loose-fitting outfit for general use. Each soul has its own special aura colour, which shows what stage of development they have attained. The colour of any garments people wear matches their aura.

As souls we represent the sum total of all our past experiences. So, in spirit we tend to present ourselves much as we looked in our last lifetime, but while we may have died infirm and elderly, in spirit we are in the full bloom of health, generally when we looked our best, often appearing as we would have been at about 30 years of age.

Interestingly, in astrology 29 years of age represents a full cycle of Saturn in each earthly life, when we become a fully fledged adult. Astrologers also regard this stage of life as a rite of passage.

Our appearance in spirit is able to be altered simply by the power of thought. However, if a soul is communicating with a loved one through a medium, they will usually present the image that people on earth are familiar with. After all, if you described someone who passed over aged 90 as appearing young, vital and active, it may be hard for us to accept that this was our deceased friend or relative, or recognise them!

In the very high spheres, souls are perceived more as orbs of light, as they have progressed beyond the need for a human appearance. These are often the same orbs seen more and more on earth. When these higher souls descend to the lower levels to help other souls heal and learn, they may assume a human form once again, simply to help others accept them more easily.

A common question that many people ask about the afterlife is, 'Can I still eat and drink there?' The short answer is yes. You can manifest anything from a cup of tea to a roast dinner served with a fine wine, but it has no substance as such. Sustenance is no longer necessary. Once the importance of eating and drinking fades, you no longer have need of it. The food and drink consumed by someone in spirit has no real effect on them, and eating can be merely a habit or simply for pleasure. Similarly, you can drink as much alcohol as you like but you won't get drunk or addicted because it doesn't have that effect.

Things like smoking or drugs do not exist in the realms of spirit, but souls may appear to be smoking as this was part of a previous image. Some souls may 'smoke' when they first arrive in the afterlife to help them adjust. This is just a temporary situation and the craving soon disappears.

People arriving in spirit are usually greeted with some kind of meal, or in Brian's case afternoon tea, to make them feel comfortable. It is rather like welcoming a guest to your house and offering them coffee and a biscuit, even if you don't really want it yourself. It is done out of politeness and this habit carries over into the next world, for a time. Apparently some people in the lower spheres never really let these old habits die, but it is their choice.

Not having a physical body means there are, of course, no illnesses, no aches and pains, no bodily functions to accommodate and, apart from the healing centres for new arrivals, there are no hospitals. However, those passing over with mental or extreme emotional conditions are given any necessary help by specialist healers.

When souls first arrive they may be directed to those places in which they are most comfortable, such as with people of a familiar nationality or religion. As souls develop and advance, previous conditions such as their station in life, their religion and nationality are forgotten, as souls integrate in the oneness of spiritual life. The afterlife has been described as 'a great leveller'.

Part D
Afterlife Activities

30

Unlimited opportunities

A popular misconception of the afterlife is that we float about on clouds, dressed in gossamer-thin garments, playing a harp or some other celestial instrument. Who knows where that idea stemmed from? While it may sound idyllic in our stressful lives, we would be bored rigid with that kind of existence. Most of us in the 21st century need to be amused and entertained.

Again, the concept of 'as above, so below' applies here as in many aspects of the spirit world. So just as there are thousands of activities we can occupy ourselves with on earth, so too it is on the other side.

The possibilities in the afterlife are endless. For starters the environment is superb, in a domain that is rich in magnificent colours. Many of these colours we cannot imagine in our very limited minds. American medium Sylvia Browne was told by her guide Francine to visualise the most beautiful sight she could imagine and then multiply it one hundred times, to even come close to what the world of the afterlife is like.[1]

Not only are the colours more vibrant, nature is more abundant and magnificent. Francine went on to say that this world also contains every animal imaginable, past and present, and they live here together in peace and harmony. One of the many surprises is that our pets are waiting for us on the other side. So, you had better always be nice to that cat or dog of yours!

As I was putting the finishing touches to this afterlife exploration, my beloved cat Apollo was hit by a vehicle and passed away. I was devastated as we were very close. Animal communicator Trisha McCagh was able to contact him a short time later, and he sent me some very meaningful messages about connecting in the afterlife. He told me that his death was no accident, and we both have important work to do before we can meet again. I found this very comforting, if a little strange at first. Trisha had helped me several times to successfully communicate with Apollo when he was alive. I hadn't understood at first what he was saying from spirit, but his messages finally all came together in my heart.

One well-known artist I connected with on behalf of his widow, said he is still painting after passing over. He is obviously enjoying the rich colours of the next world. He showed me a vision of himself standing, painting in a lush garden with the reddest of red roses in the background. It was a beautiful scene, and he was sublimely happy. He often visits his wife and will meet her when she passes, but right now he is happy to keep painting. He also has his dog from boyhood days with him for company.

When we do pass over we also meet up with people from our past. Yet despite the feelings of peace and unconditional love in the world of spirit, we are not expected to embrace all and sundry. Once again the concept of free will comes into play and we can choose those with whom we wish to associate. Of course, once we reach the higher levels, the love and acceptance of everyone becomes easier to understand and embrace.

Just as there are many levels in the afterlife, there are also lots of different places we can see once we have reunited with our soul group. I have already described the classical Greek-style building Brian went to when he met with the Council of Elders. There is every type of building and dwelling you can imagine in the world of spirit, just as there is in earthly life.

People on earth are slowly coming to terms with the concept of thought creating reality, so it is hardly surprising this concept applies in the afterlife. However, on certain lower levels of attainment where the power of thought does not come into play as easily, many people still build their houses in the traditional way. Not everyone at these levels can create by thought. It has to be learned. There is of course no money, so everything is done for personal satisfaction and a sense of purpose. This concept applies at whatever level we have reached. Those who decide to design and build do so because they choose, not because of obligation or reward.

Work is not linked to survival as it is on earth, so we can choose to be bone idle if we wish. After a while, however, that, too, loses its appeal. Most people feel the need to have some kind of occupation or activity. Many choose to continue the work they did on earth, particularly those people in the creative arts. But whether it's gardening, sport, cooking, reading, making furniture, travelling or playing music, there is an exciting array of areas in which we can get involved.

31

Fun and entertainment

In the afterlife, relaxation, fun and entertainment are as popular as they are in our earthly lives. Concerts and music of all description, dance, comedies, human dramas, theatre, art galleries, exhibitions, lectures, debates and sports are all enjoyed. Whether we wish to be active participants or just part of the audience is up to us.

Those who have always wanted to write, compose, act, paint and so on are able to study these crafts, and create in whatever capacity they choose. It does not matter what we did while we were on earth, everybody is equal in the afterlife. There is no interview panel preventing us from participating.

The former actor Lionel Barrymore spoke through the famous medium Leslie Flint many years ago, to reveal that all the classical plays were produced in his sphere, and certain morality plays were performed for those in lower levels, as part of their advancement. Famous composers and playwrights who are in the afterlife continue to create new works which are performed widely. Those who love playing or watching sport are well catered for in the afterlife.

Michael Roll is the founder of the British group investigating 'the case for secular survival'.[1] His encounters with the departed include direct contact with a wide range of people via physical mediums, who are able to help in the materialisation of spiritual entities.

In a very emotional session he was able to connect, touch and converse with his departed father, who materialised and sat next to him for some considerable time. In another encounter, Michael tells of communicating with Sir Oliver Lodge, the famous scientist and pioneer of radio broadcasting. He fired a series of questions about life on the other side at Sir Oliver, who had materialised in the room. Michael is a keen sportsman, a golfer as well as a rugby and cricket enthusiast, and wanted to know whether we can still enjoy sport once we pass over.

Sir Oliver replied, 'Michael, what makes you think we don't play sport in the other world? Of course we do, because our world over here is just as solid and as natural as yours is on earth.'

Michael was quick to point out, as far as he was concerned, that Lodge's response did not constitute scientific evidence, but he was happy to accept what Sir Oliver had said. Lodge went on to say that everything has been recorded in what they reference as 'spirit time'. This means we can go and enjoy great sporting feats and other events of the past that take our fancy. In other words, if we wish to experience a classic game of tennis, or see a past Olympic Games, we can do so. The great news is we can be part of a virtual reality audience, not just watch a video replay.

Sports activities include all ball games, tennis, golf, cricket, baseball, along with all kinds of water sports and outdoor activities such as hiking, canoeing and mountain climbing. There's also surfing, bike riding and all forms of racing, there are apparently wonderful ski slopes, and the golf courses are out of this world (pardon the pun).

One of Michael's colleagues is retired lawyer Victor Zammit. Victor has taken up the case for the afterlife, presenting his evidence in a legal manner as if he were appearing in court.[2] Describing himself as an open-minded sceptic, Victor has compiled some excellent information on the afterlife. Funnily enough, he was actually a member of the sceptics association before commencing his research.

Victor listed respected spirit entities such as Silver Birch and former researcher and medium Arthur Findlay, who confirmed details of life on the other side from their perspective. They also report living in a wonderful world—a place of enormous light, peace, beauty and love—and confirm that when we pass over we adopt the apparent image of a much younger and more vital person. We are of 'a much higher frequency and so lighter than on earth'.

Arthur Findlay also mentioned what many others report from the afterlife: that the colours there are so much more vibrant, and that 'there is a kind of harmony and light we on earth cannot appreciate'.

Victor recounted the joke about the man who had passed over and was waiting impatiently for his wife to join him there, as he was missing her kisses and cuddles. He sent a message to her through a medium, that the afterlife was a wonderful place, full of love and beauty and he was having a lovely time—so, hurry up and come over. He then added that if she had not fed him that special diet to keep him healthy, he would have been there enjoying himself ten years earlier!

But it is not all fun and games. Bruce Moen, a former engineer turned afterlife explorer, has compiled extensive research that looks at how we expand our education and learning in the afterlife. He recorded these observations:

As I've been gathering material for my books, I've discovered there is more to the non-physical world than just an afterlife existence for humans. There are also other realms to explore and learn about.[3]

He also discovered that the afterlife, like the physical world, is a school we are all attending, in the continuing evolution of our consciousness. Just as we came to the physical world to increase our understanding of who and what we are, we return to the afterlife with the opportunity to continue our learning.

All in all, it would seem the afterlife for many is at first like a wonderful holiday resort. No wonder it is called paradise. However, like all holidays it does not last forever, and there *is* work to be done, classes to attend and future lives to plan.

32

Is there sex over there?

Sex plays such a prominent role in our lives on earth it is hardly any surprise that this is one of the most frequently asked questions about the afterlife.

The short answer is yes, there is sex in the afterlife. The more detailed reply is that it is not the same sexual experience we have on earth, as of course the afterlife is a non-physical realm.

When you think about it, the Creator Spirit gave us a wonderful gift in sex. It is after all primarily the means for the human race to propagate, but what a delightful way to achieve population growth. The sexual act is far more than for propagation purposes, of course, and can be a beautiful reflection of the love between two people. Some very fortunate people on earth discover their physical joining can also include the merging of their spirits. This is an unforgettable experience.

It is hardly surprising that this spiritual merging is also present in our life in the world of spirit. A couple of years after Judy passed over we met in the dream state and what started out as a loving hug turned into something far more momentous. It really felt as if we had become one energy, one being. Words cannot express the emotion I felt. Jo Buchanan, a highly experienced metaphysician and healer, told me this is referred to as 'melding' on the other side.

Sylvia Browne's guide, Francine, told her there is both sexual and non-sexual melding, and referred to it as 'merging'. Francine described the sexual merging as a powerful orgasm, the depth, length and intensity of which we cannot imagine on earth.[1] She also said when this melding is shared in the spirit of unconditional love, it becomes more widespread and not simply between partners or soul mates. On the other hand, non-sexual merging involves entering into the essence of another soul for a complete sharing, pleasurable experience, creating a mental and emotional high.

There is no evidence of jealousy in spirit, despite the fact that over the course of many lifetimes we have all had numerous partners, some of whom we may meet up with again. When married partners cross over, they do not necessarily reunite on the other side. It depends on their soul relationship and development.

I was blessed with a rare contact with Judy while completing this book. She informed me that there are normally no restrictions on relationships in the afterlife. As such, marriage, as we understand it, is unnecessary and people are together through choice. There is no jealousy where she is now residing, in what she describes as the fifth level. 'Spirits, being androgynous, live together in peace and harmonious companionship, with no need for artificial boundaries and restrictions,' she told me.

So married partners on earth do not necessarily live together and continue their relationship in the afterlife—it is their personal choice. As we are reunited with people from past lives once we return 'home', no matter which level we are on, several spirits can choose to live together in a state of unconditional love with no petty jealousies to create problems.

A previous guide informed me that my own mother and father now live a great distance apart in the spirit world, despite being extremely close while they were alive, even sharing the same birthday. I have had some contact with my father, who is apparently now working as a spirit guide, however I have not been able to contact my mother, except for one occasion when she visited briefly and sat on the end of my bed. No words or thoughts were exchanged, but I did feel her love. M tells me she has now reincarnated somewhere in South America.

The concept of a soul mate or even twin soul is also an interesting one. While we have many soul 'mates', as in our soul family, the whole idea of being attached to only one soul energy throughout eternity has been romanticised. Once again it boils down to individual choice or free will.

The twin soul concept means one soul has split, often into two parts. Sometimes it can split into more parts for growth experiences on earth and in other worlds. Once reunited, the twin souls merge again into the one energy. This can explain the incredible attraction two people can have for each other initially. However, it doesn't always result in a lifetime partnership as both souls may be seeking different experiences. Identical twins usually share the same soul energy, split into two bodies. Advanced souls are also able to split their energy during reincarnation to further and intensify their experiences.

Through the ages, the belief in the afterlife went hand in hand with the understanding that there was sex after death. Egyptian graves reveal that many male mummies had false penises strapped to them, while the females often had artificial nipples attached, as they believed these body parts were necessary in the afterlife if they wanted to have sex.

Over the course of our many lives on earth, we experience lives as both male and female, so it makes sense that we would meld or merge with many different spiritual energies on the other side. We recognise each other in the non-physical world as an individual soul, and not as a man or a woman. As we are all spiritual beings enjoying a human experience, if the soul recognition runs deep in us all, does it really matter about our gender? The love between two souls is far more important in the long run.

33

Religion and the afterlife

In all my research into the afterlife I have not found one shred of evidence to support the existence of any kind of religion there. Many people I have spoken to or channelled from the afterlife all report the same thing. As far as they know, there is no religion practised or even referred to in the spirit world. While sceptics may argue that I am only connecting with non-religious souls, these contacts were from average, everyday people.

Nancy Canning, a between-lives regressionist, has helped countless people to access their afterlife experiences and confirms that not one of her subjects has reported any knowledge of religion in their regressions. She, too, has found religion is a non-issue. 'It never gets brought up [in their regression]. In the spirit world there is no religion, because that is part of the human experience and not part of the spiritual experience,' she maintains. Nancy found even when very religious people, such as bishops, nuns, prophets and rabbis, return to the spirit world they were not greeted by a religious figure such as Jesus or Buddha, but were instead met and welcomed by their guide or members of their soul family.

The existence of angels is entirely another matter. Contact with angelic beings seems to be widespread, both on earth and in the world beyond. Several months before she passed over, Judy told me about a dream in which she was visited by an angelic presence who gave her the choice of staying in a pain-wracked body or returning to spirit.

The angelic realm is believed to be in a much higher dimension than we are able to access. Angels have the freedom to move through all the dimensions, and may appear in many forms, from a sphere of light to the traditional robed figure with wings. Angels are also able to take the form that is most appropriate for the people they are with at the time.

Highly religious souls usually find themselves in a familiar religious setting when they first return to the world of spirit, to help ease their return and make them feel comfortable. In effect they have created this image of the afterlife from their strongly held belief system. Those who believe a pious life will see them in a kind of pre-conceived heaven will find themselves in that setting. They do not realise at first there is any other kind of life outside this, however, they are eventually shown gently that other spiritual levels are open to them if they choose to advance into them. There is no pressure exerted on these souls as it is up to each individual to decide when to progress.

This sphere is located on the Plane of Illusion, and is a self-contained area to correspond with the beliefs and practices of very religious people. There are many specialised sections, and people do not generally mix with other religions. Victor Zammit describes this as 'hollow heaven', a place where like-minded souls with rigid beliefs find themselves.[1] He says some people are so fixed in their beliefs that they stay in this place waiting for Mohammad, Jesus, Buddha, Jehovah—or whoever they believe will come for them—to arrive and spirit them away to paradise. Victor found even these souls eventually understand the afterlife is much more than they imagined. He spoke of the level or vibration of the soul as being the key for their advancement to the higher levels. We create our soul level by our deeds in our life on earth. Those who lead a positive life, helping others and learning valuable lessons, will achieve a higher vibration than those who kill, maim and destroy, or lead a dissolute life.

Victor talks of the universal laws of cause and effect in which we reap what we sow. Cause and effect is also part of our karma, so any actions that cause harm and misery have to be redressed, and this can take many future lifetimes to balance. At the lower end of the vibration scale, religious fanatics who take lives or destroy those who do not share their beliefs will find themselves at a level that corresponds with the vibration they have created for themselves.

Victor also mentions what he terms 'the laws of progress', which offer every soul the opportunity to evolve. Dogmatic beliefs can affect our progress in the afterlife but, as with everything spirit, we are never without hope or help.

Victor saw a TV interview with US presenter Larry King on this subject which provided a graphic example of rigid beliefs. A fundamentalist Christian spokesman postulated that after death we either 'go into the presence of God, or leave it forever'. These fear tactics can have profound effects on those who are unwilling or unable to open their minds. On the same program a Catholic priest was much closer to the truth when he maintained that we do not have to be a Christian to go to heaven, that it all depends on the way we live our life. It does not matter whether we are Jewish, Hindu, Muslim or whatever, our devotion to God and spirit is what really counts.

34

Just another day in paradise

Robert Murray, a Canadian medium and retired school teacher, regularly channels messages from the other side. Bob has written the story of his late son-in-law, Michael, who died in a car accident in 1997.[1] It tells a heartwarming tale of a young man who found himself returning to the world of spirit before he expected it. Michael was embraced by a warm community and, as a former entertainer, created his own reality where he found himself in the company of some well-known showbiz people who had banded together.

Communities such as this are to be found in various parts of the afterlife, especially in those spheres closer to earth. People often find comfort in being with those they can associate with, whether it is for reasons of occupation, religious belief, race or colour. Then, after a certain interval, they often choose to move on to experience different groups and activities.

Michael had been an Elvis impersonator back on earth and was delighted to be in the company of those who were still putting on shows and concerts for a whole new audience. Without the worry of investors, star salaries, theatre hire and ticket sales, creative people were able to simply work for the love of it.

He started helping in the production area, then eventually found his way into performing. This was something that had previously been Michael's greatest ambition. Imagine his shock when he finally got to meet his idol, Elvis, who was now working with young children and who then invited Michael to work with him. Elvis is apparently a very different person now, more interested in helping others to adjust to their new life, putting his days as a rock star well behind him. However, he still does the occasional performance for his spirit audience.

Michael comes through regularly from the afterlife, communicating with Bob and describing all manner of activities he's involved in, as well as daily life in the spirit world. While at last communication Michael was working with children of all ages who have passed over and helping them to reconnect with family and loved ones, he has a questing mind and often explores many other areas of the afterlife in his search for knowledge.

After at first struggling to adjust to his new conditions, Michael finally learned how to transport himself around the world of spirit using the power of thought, which he refers to as 'zapping'. At first he did this by conjuring up a vision of earthly forms of transport to get around, but once he mastered the thought process, he was easily able to move instantly from his home base to other levels and areas to which he has been given access, and has even been able to visit another planet.

A recent message he sent through to Bob concerned the question of what happens to terrorists and suicide bombers when they arrive on the other side:

Last year many people arrived over here, some were famous and others weren't so. Of course, fame is fleeting and only counts on earth when you're alive, so to speak. Once you're over on this side, it doesn't matter how famous you were back home. So, fame is fleeting. So are notorious people and that depends on who's counting. In some places they have become martyrs while in other places they're terrorists. If those modern martyrs only knew what awaited them, they wouldn't be so anxious to die.

I can tell you for certain that those people, those misguided martyr/terrorists, don't get special treatment when they arrive on this side. Crowds of well-wishers, lush tropical gardens, dancing virgins or any special treatments don't await them. Now, I haven't seen all of them arrive but I did see one arrive just last week. Amid [not his real name] crossed over after blowing himself up in a car in Afghanistan. He also brought over some adults and children. The children were greeted by relatives and helpers. Family and special greeters awaited the adults. Amid was met by a lone member of his former political group. He was led away to a barren campsite that was populated by others who had killed themselves for their beliefs. They lived in tents, ate basic food and all were looking very dejected when I walked in.

I was curious about many things. Nobody refused me entry to their campsite, and I used thought language to communicate. Because I had seen Amid arriving, I wanted to find out what his story was. Mostly, I wanted to know what made him do what he did. I didn't want to get inside his head, but I was curious as to what made him take such a drastic step. What promises were made to him? What or who convinced him to take the very drastic measure of not only killing himself, but also bringing others over with him?

At first he didn't want to deal with me. I just kept at him until he started responding. At first he made it clear that he hated me. My answer to that was that he didn't know enough about me to hate me. He implied that I was a devil, but at least he was communicating. He blamed me for his trip over here. He claimed I was responsible for all the trouble in the world and all the misery back on earth. I pointed out that he was the one who blew himself up, just in case he had missed the point.

Others in the camp gathered to witness the argument. They wanted me to go away and leave them alone. I'm ashamed to say that I lost my temper and indicated that I had as much right to be on that barren desolate place as they had. I quickly amended my behaviour to show them that I had a much better place to live, and that I wouldn't help them to improve their own campsite unless they behaved properly. After all, they couldn't throw me out the door, because they didn't have a door.

I questioned them about their hospitality. Why didn't they offer me something to eat and drink? Some of them hustled about and brought me a hot cup of tea along with some flat bread. We then sat down together around a small fire. I was on the ground with only a thin blanket under me. The others were on the ground.

They wanted to know where I lived, and what I did to deserve a fine house.

I had shown some pictures of where I live now. I explained how I was able to share a very large house with friends. I tried to convince them that they, too, could live in very large houses if they so wished. They didn't believe me and felt that they deserved to live on stony ground in [draughty] tents.

After communicating for what seemed like hours, they admitted that they had done things that had deemed them to be unworthy and were waiting until someone gave them pardon or some such thing. I was really tempted to stand up right there and give a pardon to them all. I even managed to inform them that they were going to wait a long time before anyone came along and blessed them, at least as far as I knew. They were stuck, not only in time but in their own minds.

As far as I could tell, from the limited time I had with them, they were not cruel, vicious or mean about anything. They, when alive, were convinced that they were doing the only thing possible to drive out the 'infidels'. In some cases they were not even from the country where they blew themselves up.

Some were drugged when they ended their lives. Most of them were high on something when they committed the final act. A really sad bunch, the whole lot of them.[2]

This is a really interesting account, which hints at how we can get stuck in our version of things even in the afterlife. No form of violence is acceptable in this world or the next, as it goes against the natural oneness of life. Obviously, these poor souls would have been given spiritual help and guidance from higher levels as soon as they were open to it. This is something I'm familiar with because of my experiences as Brian. All in all though, it is a sobering message for all those who would do harm to their fellow human, whether they be terrorists or otherwise.

When I asked Bob Murray for permission to use this story, he was quick to point out that mass murder is certainly not limited to the Middle East. Sadly it has been prevalent throughout history. And in more recent times there have been a number of cults whose leaders urge them to violent and destructive acts against society and themselves. The Jonestown massacre in 1978 is a classic example of this. Nine hundred and nine people died after drinking, or being force-fed, cyanide-laced grape juice.

These types of deluded souls have to then undergo extensive spiritual cleansing and deep reflection before they are able to move to the next stage of their soul's journey. Michael also indicates those who have suicided are often very lonely, isolated figures.

In a much earlier afterlife regression, I found myself sitting all alone on a desolate, windy mountaintop. I, too, experienced a disturbing feeling of deep isolation and intense loneliness. It was a chilling experience. Reflecting on this, the message came through strongly that I had needed to spend a lot of time reflecting on the life I had just lived, which was why I was alone. During my regression I was given no inkling of the events of that life, but I realised my actions must have had a pretty dramatic effect for me to end up all alone on that mountain. My guide M has since confirmed that I took my own life, and so I needed to reflect on what had happened before I could move on.

One thing I now know for sure after that experience is that I never want to find myself back in that place of isolation again.

35

A fisherman's story

Each person's experience of the afterlife is unique. Several years ago I was helping my friend Kelly Dale develop his medium skills. At the time he was a member of my spiritual development group. Kelly is a very talented trance medium,[1] so with a minimum of effort, I was able to guide him in his travels through the world of spirit.

His guide, Ossius, had a very powerful influence in Kelly's development process and was always with him during these sessions. One of Kelly's journeys into the spirit world found him connecting with a man called Tony, a rough diamond who worked on boats, back in the 1960s and 70s. Tony knew he had passed over around 1980, so by the time he encountered Kelly he had been on the other side for quite some time.

When asked what he was doing now, Tony replied, 'I'm over here, learning and stuff, but I was never a great learner.' Tony had apparently left school at 14 in his last life and went to work on boats. While he was obliged to attend classes in spirit, he was bored by the whole process. Apart from classes Tony did the same kind of things he did on earth. He walked a lot, and said he was really pleased to see his parents and other friends who had passed over.

Tony was in the afterlife for quite a long time before he realised where he actually was. Before that, Tony remembers wandering around in a kind of limbo. He used to hang around marinas on earth because he didn't know what else to do. Tony revealed he died on board a fishing vessel about 20 kilometres out to sea. He was pulling in nets and got his arm caught in one of them during a storm and couldn't free himself. He then became tangled in the machine hauling in the nets, and that was the last thing he remembers. Tony's description of the accident was told in very salty language, the way you would expect a fisherman to tell a tale.

'Anyway,' he recalled, 'I must have hung around for a while, and then someone came down, an uncle of mine, Gary, just came out of the blue. He said to me I was in limbo, that I'd died. He brought me back up here and that's when I realised what was going on.'

Uncle Gary took Tony back to his house and that's when Tony was reunited with deceased family members. 'It was amazing, really, they were all there,' he explained. 'I cried and I hadn't cried for years. Since then I've been a bit slow on the uptake. I can go and do things, but I suppose I've always been a bit of a loner, and I'm still a bit of a loner up here.' Tony prefers his solitude and describes himself as a bit lazy, but says they are not forced to learn. It's all up to the individual. He wished they'd done that at school on earth, as he might have learned a bit more.

Tony said he often sees his parents, but that it is a lot different on the other side. He doesn't have to get into the car or catch a bus to go and see them; he just thinks about seeing them and suddenly they are there right in front of him.

Tony's parents live in another part of the spirit world, and they like to go off and 'learn things'. He went with them on several occasions as they joined thousands of other people in a large auditorium to hear various speakers and teachers. At other times, according to Tony, they just sit around with a few people in a park. 'They talk and work out things, like where they're going next and stuff like that.'

Tony admitted he was getting a bit bored with his life in spirit, and felt it could be a sign that he was getting ready to do something new. When asked if there was someone who could help him with that, he said, 'Oh yeah, there's heaps of people like that. Every second person you can go and talk to about it.'

Not surprisingly Tony had chosen to live next to the water. He said he was living in a waterfront property he could never have afforded back on earth. When I asked him how he acquired such a great house, he said when he arrived he was asked where would he like to live. Enquiring where he could afford to live, he was informed it had nothing to do with money. He had always wanted a house right on the waterfront so he could wake up each morning and look at the water. He had also dreamed of his own boat tied up at his jetty out front, which to him meant freedom.

When he was told to wish for that house now he was in the afterlife, it made him burst out laughing at the prospect, but he thought he might as well. 'It just kind of . . . appeared,' he said. 'Suddenly it was my house and that's where I live now. I'm on the water.'

Tony got his every wish, a big house by a lake and a boat. He described it as like a big holiday house, where sometimes his parents come to stay, and other friends drop in for a visit.

I asked Tony whether he had a partner or a girlfriend and he said that he had met up with Charlene, a girl he knew many years ago. He and Charlene are now living together.

When I broached the delicate subject of sex, Tony told me there was sex where he was, 'and plenty of it'. He seemed a little embarrassed, then explained that it was not like sex on earth. 'It's kind of hard to explain,' he said. 'You kind of touch and stuff, but then you kind of "mould in" with each other's body. It's funny, but it's great. Sometimes you don't have to do anything. You can just be touching each other gently. It's pretty good.'

When I asked Tony if he knew whether he would be returning to earth at some future stage, he said he had been told he would be coming back a number of times. He'd already had a few lives, but had not been told when he was going to reincarnate. He was enjoying his present life, even though he was ready for some new activities, and had no real desire to return. He didn't know whether he had to ask to return or whether he would be sent back but assumed he would find out later.

Tony said he didn't have to work but was able to please himself and do whatever he enjoyed. When I asked about the need for sleep in the afterlife, Tony described the process as more like resting rather than sleep as we understand it.

'I do lie down and kind of close my eyes,' he told me. At this stage he was struggling to explain the process in terms I could understand. 'You know sometimes when you go to sleep and you suddenly open your eyes and you've had half an hour but you could swear it was only a couple of minutes? Well, it's kind of like that, I just close my eyes and then open them, and it's like I've had 12 hours sleep.'

I also asked Tony about recreation and entertainment. 'There's non-violent movies just like the same ones you see back on earth, and sports like cricket and football, and a couple of other games I've never seen,' he explained. 'There's also kids who've passed over, playing games and laughing. There doesn't seem to be any kind of anger or violence. Maybe there is, but I haven't seen any. There's just a really good feeling here, really loving.'

Tony's macho image took over here as he got quite embarrassed about the feeling of loving that was everywhere, even amongst 'the blokes'. The feeling I got from communicating with Tony was that of a very comfortable and beautiful world. The kind of image, I guess, we could easily accept as 'heaven'.

36

Furthering our knowledge

So what was happening for Brian? Further past-life regressions revealed that he felt a sense of satisfaction and peace as he settled into the spirit world. During this time he thought about the message from the Council of Elders about the folly and futility of war, and could see how right they were. Now that he had truly learned this lesson over many lifetimes he could look forward to new experiences in his next return to earth.

After resting, recuperating and reconnecting with our soul families, our 'work' schedule begins. But it's not the sort of work we're used to on earth. Returning souls are expected to attend group sessions where we look back in great detail over our last life with the aid of our guides and other group members. Here, we analyse where we succeeded and where we fell short of expectations. These learning opportunities are an essential part of the inter-life development for each soul.

Everyone comes back to earth with certain personal goals to achieve. Many of these goals involve karmic issues, which help us balance out previous experiences. So, instead of being childless in our new life we get to experience parenting, the rich often return in poor circumstances, thieves may return as someone who loses everything through robbery, and so on. Karma is not vengeance, as many imagine. It is simply experiencing the other side of the coin. We are on earth to learn as much about life as possible through our many lifetimes. These lessons may include sorting out prior relationship issues, resolving and releasing blockages from past lives, often involving forgiveness, helping others in their spiritual journey and, of course, learning more lessons about ourselves.

Each soul gets to know its purpose in its next life on earth. Once the soul is in a new body, this knowledge is blocked, as a veil is lowered at birth to allow that new life to unfold. While this mightn't seem fair, we need a fresh uncluttered mind to exercise the free will given to us. Those memories of the goals for our new life are locked in our subconscious and can be accessed in a variety of ways, if our guides deem it appropriate. Meditation and regression help us access the subconscious; however, there are also other intuitive methods available to us, such as through dreams. Simply asking for guidance can also open many doors.

Once we are back in the spirit world, the veil that was placed over us dissolves, and we are able to remember what we set out to achieve and experience in the life just completed. Group discussions and activities can be very intense in the afterlife, but are always in the best interest of each soul. We are also able to review our past lives, and this information is available to us in our development classes.

As the group, along with their various guides, meets, events are replayed and analysed. All the options around each situation are discussed, so we can learn by our mistakes. It's rather like after a sporting event, where the team sits down with the coach to dissect the various parts of the game, to help them lift their performance for the next match.

Returning home to the spirit world does not automatically mean we suddenly have the wisdom of the universe. If someone is not too bright during their life on earth, chances are they will still be that way in the afterlife. Basically we are the sum total of all our past experiences, including our past lives.

So, while you may hope that when your Uncle Fred or Aunt Mary passes over they will be able to communicate a rich source of useful information to help you back on earth, you may be disappointed. The best advice is, if you took note of what they had to say when they were alive, then go ahead and listen to their messages. Otherwise, be very careful.

However, as with all aspects of life, nothing is completely black and white. Appearances can be deceptive. While some souls do accumulate a depth of wisdom and knowledge over various lifetimes, they may have agreed to lead a simple life in their last earthly incarnation for a variety of reasons. They could be spirit guides returning to earth as observers, or perhaps updating their earthly experiences if they haven't reincarnated for many years. They could also be there to interact and help in the growth of other souls, or their decision could be a karmic one. These advanced souls are the exception to the rule.

Past-life expert Peter Ramster filmed a number of people from all different walks of life who he regressed, catapulting them back into a former life on earth.[1] It turned out to be not always their immediate past life. After their regressions Peter took them back to the location of their previous life to follow up his investigation.

His best subject, Gwen McDonald, was able to provide some breathtaking details of her past while under hypnosis. Gwen described a life in a hamlet near Glastonbury in 18th-century England, which she referred to as St Michael's Abbey. When Peter arrived in the district his research proved she was correct. Gwen also described the house in which she had lived in that lifetime, providing some intricate details of the colour of the floor tiles and the stonemason's mark on each tile. These descriptions were later checked and found to be completely accurate, much to the amazement of Peter's film crew.

Gwen had never been to England in her current life. Peter told me Gwen was leading a very simple existence but, when regressed, revealed amazing knowledge gained over many different lifetimes. Gwen has since passed over. Peter was convinced that despite the simplicity of her life just gone, Gwen was a very advanced soul. He later received several messages from her in the afterlife which confirmed this belief.

37

The Hall of Records

'Akasha is one of the cosmic principles and is a plastic matter, creative in its physical nature, immutable in its higher principles. It is the quintessence of all possible forms of energy—material, psychic or spiritual—and contains within itself the germs of universal creation, which sprout forth under the impulse of the Divine Spirit.'

HELENA BLAVATSKY, *Alchemy and the Secret Doctrine* (1927)

Meanwhile Brian was progressing on his inter-life journey. In yet another regression I watched on as Brian revisited the Hall of Records, also often referred to as the Cosmic Library, where every life, every deed, is recorded. This time the visit was for a private session. Markus escorted him to this session without any prior warning. In the higher levels of the world of spirit there are no cars, buses, trains or planes—people either walk or 'think' themselves to wherever they want to be. It is rather like hearing the doorbell ring and knowing we need to go to the front door. The thought creates the action, which then happens automatically, without you having to concentrate on getting your legs to move.

After Markus unexpectedly arrived, one moment Brian was at home, the next he was in a large building, which seemed to stretch away into the distance forever. Although he had been there with his soul group beforehand, this time being in the Hall of Records felt very different for Brian. The place was humming with activity and, despite not actually seeing anybody, he distinctly felt their presence around him.

He and Markus went into a private area, not a room as such, more like a secluded space, and made themselves comfortable. By now Brian was starting to remember past visits to the Hall of Records, and the procedure came back to him without any prompting. He recalled that there were a number of ways to see the records of his past deeds. Your expectations determine how the information is provided for you. So, if you expect to see long lines of shelves stacked with ancient scrolls and dusty manuscripts, or a computer screen, then that is how your previous lives will be presented to you.

As Brian had a very open and curious mind, he was taken back many lifetimes to the dim, distant past with a series of images in his mind's eye. The images then spooled forward, in a series of what are best described as flashbacks.

As fleeting as they were, Brian was able to instantly review each of his lives and take in what learning he needed from it, to help him with his next life.

The thing that stood out as he reviewed the people he had been in the past was that he had had a lot of lives as a man, but only a few as a woman. This, of course, does not necessarily mean he had more male lives, just that he needed to see these lives at this stage.

After Brian's previous session with the Council of Elders it was hardly surprising that a lot of these lives depicted him as various kinds of warriors. One life, in particular, stood out from the others. He saw himself as a Norse warrior named Ulrich, a large, violent man who revelled in plundering, killing and raping. This was a short, but colourful life.

After that, he was shown a few of his lives as a woman. One in particular stayed with him, where he suffered very badly when his town was invaded. Markus gently explained Brian had a karmic debt to repay, and had to experience the kind of violence he had dealt out as Ulrich.

Brian also revisited more spiritual lives as a priest or shaman, ranging from ancient Egyptian times to the middle ages. He was shown images of one life as a priest in Dendera in ancient Egypt, and another as a shaman, or Kahuna, in the Hawaiian Islands. Markus explained this was an important change of direction for Brian as a soul.

Much to Brian's surprise he also saw himself as a nun in Southern France in the 16th century, battling the unwanted attentions of a visiting priest.

When Brian had completed his visionary excursion through previous existences, Markus said he needed to review these lives as the first step in preparing for his next incarnation on earth. Brian was naturally curious to find out more about how his new life would unfold, but was told it would all be revealed in the soul group sessions.

The Cosmic Library or Akashic Records remarkably contain far more than just each individual's past-life details. They actually go all the way back to the time when the earth was first formed and then chronicle every event, every thought, that has taken place throughout history. Once granted access to the Hall of Records, it is possible to not only visit your own past, but tune in to any period in history.

The full extent of the Akashic Records seems to be one of the mysteries we cannot fully grasp due to our limited thinking. The degree of access permitted to us depends on the level to which the individual soul has attained. It would seem the majority of people are primarily permitted to access their own past lives and actions, which are viewed in the company of a guide, who helps them in their understanding and knowledge of themselves and their future direction.

Canadian medium Bob Murray's son-in-law Michael, who we talked about earlier, describes the Akashic Records as life albums, confirming we can only access them when we are ready to deal with the information. Over time a world of knowledge and wisdom becomes available to us. As a musician Michael was very excited at entering the Hall of Records, because he could also listen live to any piece of music ever written or played. Some 'exhibits', according to Michael, come alive and are displayed as holographic images.

There are many references to the Akashic Records through history, in folklore, in myth, and in both the Old and New Testaments. In Exodus 32:32 we read, after the Israelites had sinned by worshipping the golden calf, Moses pleaded to God for mercy on their behalf, offering to take full responsibility and have his own name stricken 'out of thy book which thou hast written'. In Psalm 139, David describes the fact that God has written down everything about him and all the details of his life, 'in your book' for all past thoughts and deeds and also those 'not yet formed'.

There was widespread belief among ancient peoples, such as the Assyrians, the Babylonians and the Phoenicians, that the history of mankind was carved on celestial tablets along with spiritual information. Druidic priests in Ireland, Scotland, Wales and England were reputed to access the Akashic Records.

Edgar Cayce, the 'sleeping prophet', was able to tune into the Records during the readings he gave, which he described as coming from the 'Book of Life'. He talked of the records as 'the storehouse of all information for every individual who has ever lived upon the earth, containing every word, deed, feeling, thought, and intent that has ever occurred'. Cayce also believed that by looking into the records we are able to shape the course of our destiny.

When we have reached a certain level in the afterlife, we are able to make many such visits to the Hall of Records to help us as we come to terms with our past lives and actions. Those in the lower astral levels are not permitted to visit this special place, as their minds are closed, or they are still lost in their past deeds. However, ours is a compassionate universe, and so these confused souls are still shown relevant visions as part of their learning, if they are likely to be open to them. At the end of each Akashic Records session, there is a customary debriefing with our guide, so we can fully understand what we have experienced. As the Akashic Records are being constantly updated, it is no wonder they are often referred to as being like a universal database.

How powerful these records must be when we are able to see and experience them, as we plan for the next part of our soul's journey.

38

Communicating with people on earth

How we get to communicate with our loved ones on earth is different for everyone. Some of us are able to return to earth immediately, others take longer. Some people are held back in their soul's journey by deeply grieving family members who don't want to let them go. Many, like Brian, needed to get themselves completely healed in spirit before such a visit. Some souls are so disenchanted with their previous life, they choose to move on without a backward thought.

Communication with those in the spirit world has been happening for thousands of years, and it is very widespread. Since the passing of my partner Judy, my own abilities as a medium have grown exponentially. I regularly contact those in the afterlife. I do this both for people who come to me for readings and for my own purposes. The majority of contact with those in the afterlife provides what is known as 'survival evidence', specific information from spirit which proves to those on earth that their loved ones are still alive and in a wonderful place. Basically the message is life goes on, we have no pain anymore, and we will see you when you get over here yourself.

Messages from those in the world of spirit are usually very simple. Information of major importance is rarely relayed, but if the medium is experienced enough, valuable advice is often available. Those in spirit often communicate with mediums by using symbols and visual references. Some mediums hear the communications, some sense it and some receive visions. I frequently receive information that means nothing to me, but when described to the person I am conducting the reading for it often makes sense to them and is usually information that only they know and understand.

In one group session I conducted, the person in spirit showed me a pair of work boots, which I was able to describe in detail. This resonated with Steve, one of the men in the group, as belonging to his deceased father. After that, the spirit told me his name was Jim, which confirmed to Steve that it was indeed his deceased father. Jim had come through to his son because he had lost contact with Steve when he was alive, and wanted to apologise. The effect on Steve was very emotional and was the catalyst for his healing.

In a more recent reading with Dianna, an Argentinian woman, her grandmother came through strongly in the session. After the opening greetings Dianna's grandmother showed me a set of stairs. When I relayed this to Dianna, she teared up as she told me that as a child her grandmother would always wave her granddaughter goodbye from the top of the stairs leading to her house. This image had always stayed with Dianna, who hated leaving her grandmother behind to return home to her own village, as it was some distance away.

Messages come through in all kinds of ways and for different purposes. Another soul showed me a red tartan scarf, which was enough to prove to her granddaughter Simone that it was indeed her beloved grandmother. All Simone's grandmother wished to convey was a feeling of love and support for her favourite granddaughter. So there were no world-shattering messages, just a simple hello from the other side, which meant a great deal to Simone.

On another occasion a man who took his own life came through to ask his family for forgiveness, as he was still healing in the afterlife. As part of his survival evidence he showed me an image of a rope. His emotional widow confirmed that he had indeed hanged himself.

There are many mediums all over the world doing wonderful work healing the broken hearts of those left behind by communicating messages from the afterlife. One of the finest I have worked with is Ezio De Angelis. Ezio receives all manner of information from the other side, often seeing a clear image of the departed soul. He is able to address the relevant members of the audience in his live appearances to pass on the appropriate messages. I worked with Ezio in several stage appearances a few years ago, and one contact will always stick in my mind. He identified the soul of an elderly man coming through from spirit with a message for a group of people at one particular table. I was in the audience with the microphone during this demonstration and went over to the table concerned. It turned out they were all members of the same family, and readily identified the spirit as their grandfather.

Ezio really blew this family away when he revealed their grandfather's bathing habits leading to his passing. They all started laughing as Ezio colourfully described the body odour of the old man, who had chosen this highly unusual way of confirming his presence. Up on stage Ezio's nose was screwed up, as he obviously got the full impact of the body odour, much to the amusement of the family.

Sometimes souls are able to communicate detailed information from the afterlife, although it seems simple survival evidence is the main aim. Marcia Quinton is a highly experienced medium who was one of Ezio's mentors when he trained at a Spiritualist church. Both Marcia and Ezio appeared on my live radio show some years ago, where we were able to take calls from listeners and pass on some very detailed information from the afterlife to them. The studio was really buzzing and the atmosphere was electric as some wonderful contacts were made.

The next day, when I went to the station, Richard, the studio manager, called me aside for a gentle rap over the knuckles. 'You really must control your guests, they were chattering away in the background during the calls,' he told me. I was really mystified about Richard's comment, as there was absolute silence in the studio as Marcia and Ezio took calls live on air from the listeners.

Having explained this to Richard, he then played me a recording of the session. And, strangely, it sounded like we had a live studio audience with us. Marcia and Ezio were delighted when I told them, as it was evidence of the spirit visitors who were all around us wanting to communicate with their loved ones on air. Richard, who was a bit sceptical about spirit contact before this, was instantly converted. He also told me the session had been recorded on a brand new log tape, so there could have been no sound overlay. Next time Marcia and Ezio came on air we had to ask the spirit audience to please keep the noise down!

In her private consultations, Marcia often has contact from spirits wanting to make amends for mistakes in their previous life. She says it is common for a message to come through from a soul unable to progress because of what they did to a loved one. It may be anything from manipulating someone, through to abuse and violence. The only way forward is recognition of the wrong that has been done, and a willingness to ask for forgiveness, so that everybody can get on with their lives.

Marcia believes this communication sometimes happens as part of a life review with the Elders. The soul then communicates with the relevant person on earth, so they can relate to the pain that has been caused. It is one thing for a soul to just see past events replayed on a screen, but in the spirit world the experience is much more intense. We can see and experience how we have hurt a person, or how we made a positive difference to their life.

Contact with the other side does not always have to be highly emotional or cathartic—it can have a much lighter touch. I was asked to make an appearance at the Starlight Festival a couple of years ago. A well-known local medium, Jason McDonald, was also due to appear at the festival when he suddenly took ill, so I was asked to fill in for him at the last minute. More than a little nervous I walked into a packed room full of expectant faces looking forward to meeting Jason, not me! But the energy in the room was powerful and my guides came through for me, so we had a wonderful session. A group of souls on the other side seemed almost desperate to make contact that afternoon.

One woman in spirit was missing her partner so badly that she could hardly wait for him to join her. She sent me the image of a mattress strapped to her back, much to the delight of the audience and the slight embarrassment of her partner. That was certainly one of the more colourful images I have received from the afterlife.

Not every spirit is champing at the bit to come through. Anyone consulting a medium needs to understand contact will only happen if the spirit is willing and available at the time. It is like ringing someone's home. People don't answer if they are off somewhere else, or don't wish to be disturbed.

While writing this book, another writer contacted me about her spiritual visitations. She spoke about a wonderful contact from her late husband, who was a motorcycle racing fanatic during his life. He used to sit up all night sometimes, watching what he laughingly termed 'the vroom-vrooms'. After he passed over she went to see a medium who said she had a message from her husband in spirit and that he wanted to let her know that he was alive and well in the spirit world, and was still watching the 'vroom-vrooms'. This writer knew it had to be her husband because that was their private terminology, which the medium did not know anything about.

As she recounted this story to me her mother suddenly came to me from spirit wearing a bright yellow scarf. This writer told me her mother always used to wear scarves when she was on earth. Her mother went on to explain the significance of the colour yellow. It was a special message to her daughter about the need to take care of her health and wellbeing. This writer and I have only ever spoken on the phone or by email, so it demonstrates how spirits get their message back to their loved ones, taking advantage of any opportunity that comes along. It also shows how departed souls do watch over us and are concerned for our wellbeing.

39
Spirit healers

While some may be reluctant to make contact, other souls in the world of spirit are constantly communicating with us, for a variety of reasons.

Whether we realise it or not, there is a lot of healing being sent to us from the spirit world, as people who have visited John of God in Brazil can confirm. A team of doctors in spirit performs thousands of both spiritual and physical operations at the Casa de Dom Inácio every week. People from all over the world have had life-changing experiences as a result, receiving healing for conditions from emotional and mental problems, through to so-called incurable diseases. I can personally vouch for these healings as I have seen them with my own eyes and also had successful 'surgery' myself. These dedicated spiritual beings work tirelessly to help us heal and open our hearts and minds to help in our spiritual growth.[1]

This is just one example of the interaction between the two worlds. Author Bruce Moen tells of visiting the Education Centre and also the Planning Centre in Focus 27, in his afterlife explorations at the Monroe Institute. While there he also went into the Hall of Bright Ideas, where all new inventions and ideas are developed. Here we discovered that once scientists in the afterlife have come up with a new concept, arrangements are made for the appropriate people on earth to be given this information, via dreams, or by seeding ideas that can suddenly pop into the mind.

40

Brian visits his earthly home

So much had happened to Brian since he had left his shattered body on that miserable battlefield but he was still concerned about his family back on earth. His guilt over leaving them must have been obvious, because Markus appeared to tell Brian he was now able to return to his family in spirit form.

So, the time had come for Brian to see how things were on earth since his passing. In my regression I was shown a bleak old day when Markus accompanied Brian on a visit to Devon. The journey back was a lot different to Brian's crossing over to the afterlife. There was no tunnel experience, he and Markus were just able to materialise on earth when they put their minds to it.

It was now the winter of 1918, more than two earth years since Brian died. The war had just ended and his wife Jenny was on a train heading north with their son

Simon. Jenny looked pale and sickly, and had obviously been through troubling times in the last two years. Brian had the sensation of floating near the roof of the carriage, as he observed Jenny and Simon. It was amazing how more than two years had slipped by, as it felt like only a few weeks since he had passed over. He felt guilty that he hadn't been back to see them in such a long time, especially when Jenny had been suffering.

Markus reminded Brian that as there is no time on the other side, what seems a few weeks can often see years pass on earth. By this stage Brian, feeling confused with the whole experience, lapsed into silence. But Markus explained he had been keeping an eye on Brian's family, along with Jenny's guide, so was able to quickly bring him up-to-date and reassure him.

After the events in France, Jenny had gone to live with a cousin in Taunton, as she could not afford to stay in their village in Devon. However, her cousin only had a small place, and as it was very cramped this wasn't a long-term solution.

Jenny's parents had both passed over some years beforehand, but at least she still had her mother's sister, Maude, who then insisted that Jenny come to live with her and her husband Tom. Tom and Maude lived in a village on the outskirts of Liverpool and had no children of their own, so there was plenty of space for Jenny and Simon.

When the war ended Tom had secured a good position in the office of a Liverpool flour mill. With so many young men buried on the battlefields, women were now filling all sorts of roles in the workforce, so Tom managed to get a job for Jenny at the mill.

After the long and arduous train trip, Jenny and Simon were met at the railway station by these two generous people. For the first time since returning to earth Brian felt some relief that things would turn out well for his wife and son in their new home.

When they were back in the spirit world, Brian told Markus that now Jenny and Simon were safe and sound, he had no immediate desire to return to earth. However, he did want to look in on his earth family from time to time, as he realised Jenny would cross over soon and wanted to keep an eye on Simon. Markus agreed, but added it was important Brian did not interfere in their lives and also had to observe their privacy. If Brian felt the need to visit and it was appropriate, it would be arranged. Markus told Brian that he would be able to return at various stages in his son's life. These might be quite different periods of Simon's life, as there was no such thing as a straight line of time. He also explained we are able to go back to earth to various times, as ultimately past, present and future is all one. Markus described this phenomenon as being like 'a giant loop'. Though confused, Brian was very pleased when they left the earth plane and returned home to his seaside village and his soul family. Brian would soon see Jenny again and, with his son being cared for, he could enjoy his new life.

41

Are we being watched from afar?

Some people are really nervous that our loved ones in spirit could be watching us when we least expect it. The thought of a departed parent popping in when we are enjoying a night of passion, or a deceased relative peering over our shoulder checking our work, is enough to give anyone the jitters.

Once again the answer is, 'as above, so below'. When they were alive your parents would have respected your privacy and never have barged into your bedroom without permission; the same applies in the spirit world. If you have nosy or rude friends or relatives on the other side, they would have been the same in your earthly life. If, however, you are concerned about your privacy, connect with your guide in a meditation and request any spiritual visits are made according to your conditions.

That said, people from the spirit world do pop in unexpectedly at times. Several years ago David Thompson had been appearing on my live radio program doing some readings from the afterlife. David is a very talented British medium, and the audience loved him for his ability to pass on detailed information, and also his cockney sense of humour. After we came off air David had a personal message from my late partner Judy, who David had never met. Judy told him that the previous week I had been cleaning out some drawers in my office, and found a piece of paper connected to her. She said she was sitting next to me on the floor at the time and blew in my ear. It was just the sort of cheeky thing Judy would have done! This message took my breath away. I had indeed been cleaning out my office filing cabinet drawers the previous week and found a long lost document. It was some automatic writing, dated February 1993. It revealed there was 'a very special lady coming into my life, soon, very soon now and you will have a lot of important work to do together in a very short time'. The message was spot on as it was given to me six months before I met Judy.

This sheet of paper had been caught up with other documents, and I had not seen it for several years since moving after Judy's death. Finding the paper had given me an eerie sensation at the time. Judy also told David there was a very significant anniversary coming up soon. When

I thought about it I realised she was referring to the fifth anniversary of her death, which was only two weeks away.

Judy still comes back from time to time. She has been with me on a couple of occasions as I wrote this book. Once I actually felt my hair being ruffled slightly. When I tuned in, I discovered it was Judy letting me know she was keeping an eye on my progress. She had also sent a message several years prior through Canadian medium Bob Murray, urging me to write a book, so I guess she was encouraging me from spirit.

Our loved ones do return, not so much to keep an eye on us, but just to be a part of our life. I have often been given an image of a particular part of a person's house during a reading where, it turned out, they usually spent some quiet time. The spirit communicating in that session wanted my client to know they are often with them in this particular part of the house, as quiet times are best for communication. Quite often people also see or feel a presence at the end of the bed when they are retiring for the evening. This seems to be a favourite visiting hour; again it's when we are preparing for rest.

Spirit visitors will often announce their presence in some way. We might start thinking about them for no particular reason—their favourite perfume wafts through the room or they might even gently stroke our cheek as we sit quietly. Many people have often thought they saw something fleetingly out of the corner of their eye, only to turn quickly and see nothing. Or, so it would seem.

My grandfather Harry announced his presence on one occasion with his favourite fragrance when he was alive— tobacco. Harry was a man of the outback who used to roll his own cigarettes, which had a distinct smell about them. At one stage I was awoken in the middle of the night with the familiar smell of his cigarette smoke in my nostrils. I was going through a difficult time in my personal life, and so the next morning, as I reflected on the experience, I felt he was there to comfort me.

Other people are able to see a full presence of a loved one in front of them, and believe they have seen a ghost. Well, they may have, but when necessary the departed are sometimes able to appear to us in spirit when the need is great. This takes a lot of energy for a spirit who has passed over, as they live in a much lighter world. To be seen on earth a spirit has to be able to lower its vibrations to that of our much heavier earth plane.

Recently, my elderly aunt told me her mother's spirit had appeared in her bedroom earlier that year. When she asked her mother what the message was, she was told to look after her younger brother who lived alone and had been diagnosed with Alzheimer's. My aunt accepted this as the kind of thing her mother would do. What intrigued my aunt was that her mother, who lived to be 100, appeared looking like a beautiful 30-year-old woman, not like the wizened body she had left behind some 55 years later. As we discovered earlier, this is a common practice in the afterlife.

42

Contact in the dream state

The vast majority of people I have spoken to following the death of a loved one experience a dream about them. This may be immediately after the person's passing, or it may be quite some time down the track. There is no rule of thumb here.

These dreams can range from a fleeting appearance through to significant contact, often with a message or feeling accompanying it. My father passed over while I was in Vienna, where I had just started a short contract on Blue Danube Radio. He had been ill when I left a few weeks earlier, and I was sitting quietly in a beautiful cathedral praying for his recovery. When I looked up I saw a man taking photographs in the nave. I realised with shock it was my father. He looked just as I remembered him. As I got up to go to him, he disappeared. He was literally there one moment, gone the next. The strange thing was when

I checked the cathedral, there was no way he could have left without passing me. I discovered later this was at the time of his death thousands of miles away. I believe my father came to me to say goodbye.

My next contact with my father was about a year later while I was in Tahiti, touring with a group of journalists. I had a very vivid dream, where he and I were sitting together. This time he appeared to be young and in the prime of his life. It was a very warm and emotional experience, despite the fact that we had never really been close in life.

My friend and medium Chris Kelly also came to me in a dream shortly after he passed over. We were walking along a country road together and he assured me we would stay in contact. It was a brief chat as there were many people following behind us on that same road wanting to speak with Chris. I was left with a wonderful sense of love and peace when I woke the next morning with the dream still vivid in my consciousness. In his last life on earth, Chris was also a powerful spiritual healer who displayed all the abilities of a shaman. I feel sure he is continuing his work in the afterlife.

Quite often we do not regard these dreams as anything more than some kind of vision from our memory banks, but they are definitely real encounters.

As we discussed earlier, everyone is able to leave their body and astral travel. We do it automatically, mainly at night when the body is asleep, as the soul has no need of sleep and is constantly alert. Once free of its physical limitations, the soul is able to wander far and wide, but is always joined to the body by an invisible silver cord. If we wake suddenly the cord snaps the soul back into the body, a bit like one of those retractable tape measures.

The soul enjoys many different experiences while we are asleep: sometimes it returns to the spirit world for contact with our guide and our soul group where necessary; it can communicate with departed souls; and the soul can also interact with others on the earth plane, who may or may not be in the dream state at the time.

How often have you woken up in the morning with a solution to a problem that has been troubling you? More likely than not the higher self has provided the answer for us in the best way it can. This may be from the depths of your own subconscious, through contact with those in spirit, or even by astral research in another part of our world.

What better way, then, for the departed soul to send a message to those back on earth that they have survived so-called death and are looking and feeling great, than by coming to a loved one in a dream? I have never heard anyone say they were negatively impacted by these dream visits. To the contrary—they always have a beneficial effect.

Our dream visits home to the world of spirit can be very real and very emotionally satisfying. A couple of years after Judy passed over I had a dream which is still vivid to this day. I was visiting her on the other side where she had created her own house and was proudly showing me around. Judy was very house-proud in her last life, so this was not surprising. Feeling very exhilarated I went outside and with the power of thought manifested some snowballs, then came inside and threw them at her as if we were having a game in the snowfields. She pretended to get a bit annoyed that I was messing up her lovely house and started wagging her finger at me, and told me to clean up the mess.

I woke up suddenly and sat bolt upright in bed, tears pouring down my face. I knew without a doubt I had been with Judy in her spirit house and that we had a means of staying in contact. Nobody will ever be able to convince me otherwise.

43

Brian's earth family in trouble

With Markus's assistance Brian was able to pop back to Devon from time to time to see how his wife Jenny and son Simon were faring in Liverpool. While Simon was healthy and growing up fast, Jenny was not coping very well. Her job at the mill was exhausting and her health soon began to deteriorate. It was very frustrating for Brian to not be able to help her physically. All he could do was embrace her spiritually.

When Jenny was diagnosed with tuberculosis, Markus told Brian she would be joining them in the afterlife very soon, which left Brian with mixed feelings. On the one hand they would be reunited, but their son would be orphaned. Markus patiently explained this was what Simon had agreed to in his previous life-planning session, and that he was going to be all right.

True to Markus's word Jenny died of tuberculosis a few months later. The funeral was a quiet ceremony with only her immediate family attending. Although Jenny and Brian were not religious, her sister was a churchgoer and so Jenny was buried in the local church's graveyard. When Jenny crossed over, Brian was waiting to welcome her home. Prior to this Markus had informed Brian that Jenny was part of a nearby soul family, close to his own group.

During Jenny's afterlife healing period, Brian kept an eye on Simon and was relieved to discover that his aunt and uncle had taken over the parenting role and had decided to bring him up as their own. By now Simon was six and was doing well at school. Brian was pleased that Simon had a bright future ahead of him and that he would go on to enjoy a happy and successful life.

As Jenny's illness had been relatively brief, she emerged from the healing centre after a short sojourn and joined up with her soul family. Brian ascertained that he and Jenny had shared many lifetimes and had a very close bond. The last time they had been together was in France, just after the French Revolution, where they were poverty-stricken and childless. It seemed natural that Jenny came to live with Brian in 'the Greek village' while she settled in, but she soon informed Brian that it was not her ideal location.

Despite the fact that they were from different soul families, Brian was so happy at being reunited with her that the question of housing was no great concern. He was happy to help Jenny plan her ideal house. As she preferred country living, she wanted her home to be in open spaces, surrounded by nature instead of buildings. Jenny eventually moved in to her own house and she and Brian remained close companions, visiting each other regularly.

Part E
A Screenwriter Reports from the Afterlife

44

Contacting John Dingwell

My contact with the world of spirit has come in many interesting ways. One of the most informative was from John Dingwell, a highly respected journalist and later screenwriter and film producer, who enjoyed a fruitful and successful career. His film *Sunday Too Far Away* has been described as one of the top ten Australian films ever produced.

John and I were working in the same city in the 1960s. He was a newspaper journalist and I was a raw but keen TV presenter. We met only a few times, but I remember him as a talented writer and a happy, knockabout sort of bloke who got a lot out of life. In his later years he became very interested in spiritual matters and we discussed producing a documentary film on this subject. Unfortunately, with John's rapidly deteriorating health, it never happened.

After a very painful battle with cancer John passed over early in 2005. His passing was relatively easy because he already possessed a strong belief in the afterlife. What he found difficult was the experience of leaving this life, because of the grief for his partner and family members.

John's son Kelly, together with his wife Kristin, run the Australian Casa, a healing centre directly connected to the John of God centre in Brazil. Kelly now works with his father in spirit. When I visited Kelly and Kristin's property, John came through very strongly. Even though I had only met John a few times during his life, I was able to recognise his voice and phraseology, which was nothing like Kelly's.

John told us our contact had been approved by the powers that be in the world of spirit, and that there were between 50 and 100 souls in the small room we were using, providing the necessary energy for him to communicate with us. We had all been looking forward to this meeting and had no idea it would be as significant as it turned out, so much so that at the end of the session, Kelly, who is normally very vibrant, was completely exhausted. He took the next couple of days to recover from the experience.

According to John, whether we have a belief in the afterlife or not, when we cross over we still hold on to those very human emotions which tug at our heartstrings. His actual passing he remembers as fascinating and almost surreal, like having a very vivid, realistic dream while living it at the same time. It was the kind of dream that stays with you and still feels real long after you have woken up. John found he was watching himself go through the experience, which was fascinating. 'I completely believed what was going on in the afterlife, and in a way could step aside because the belief was so easy for me,' he told me later.

It was only after he passed over that the grief of not being able to see his family again set in. His pain was eased, however, when he was met on the other side by friends and family whom he had not seen for many years. They gave him a lot of help to settle in to his new surroundings.

John's guide appeared and of course proved invaluable to him when he felt confused. John remembers he was in a state similar to being in hospital under heavy sedation. He described the next stage as drifting in and out of consciousness. 'Obviously this is just the way I passed, and there are different stages of this,' he said. 'There being no time I couldn't give you a time frame of how long I went through that particular period.' He was coaxed out of this unconscious phase by family and friends in the afterlife, along with what he describes as other wonderful spirits and helpers from higher planes, who sat and talked to him compassionately.

There were long periods of discussion, where John was given instruction on his new life in the world of spirit. He recalls being told if he wanted to feel there was night and day he could. If he also wanted to go and learn and progress, he could be with other souls in a school-like environment.

John also mentioned some of the souls he encountered have lived lives on earth as very important and powerful people, who were well placed to help and guide others in the afterlife. 'These souls are my excitement,' he told us, 'purely for their knowledge and compassion. They don't want to be named, they were just a soul in that body for a certain time. They are wonderful souls who will come back to earth to continue learning.' It is typical for those in the afterlife to shun the limelight, as we have no ego there.

John later explained that his return to the afterlife was almost like going though a selfish stage, to get the 'poor me' feelings off his chest, so he was then ready to help others. 'You start looking outside yourself and saying "I'm OK now, so what can I do, who needs help?"' he said.

John started helping others shortly after he arrived in the afterlife. He has since been working with a lot of souls who had no belief in the afterlife, and whose passing was often very traumatic. 'Some of them have their head in their hands, and if you're talking timeframe, it would be weeks of just deep, great sorrow.' He says it often takes much work—many spirits and a lot of love and compassion, just consoling, talking and reassuring these recently arrived souls that they are safe and secure—before they can progress.

John also talked about the learning process in the spirit world, which in its simplest form is almost like high school. He sat in a traditional type of classroom because that is how he feels comfortable learning, but there were many ways to further your education.

He also said that for someone with an enquiring mind there is enough knowledge available in the afterlife to last several lifetimes. He had also been inspired by so many wonderful souls who dedicate their lives to helping others in any way they can.

John described his new life as very satisfying: 'It sounds pretty ridiculous, but I've been having a ball. It's totally not what I expected. It's surprising at every turn, more knowledge than I can poke a stick at.'

John has been fortunate to have been taught by some amazing souls who are extremely loving, generous and humble—attributes he needs to learn for his own growth. His tone took on a note of respect, even awe, when he described being with them. 'When these humble souls come into your presence, you can feel, or sense, the most amazing love and compassion. I mean, where you are floored, you are humbled. No words are spoken, but you just know the being in front of you is truly compassionate and you sit down and listen,' John said. 'I've been fortunate enough to be in the presence of a lot of these souls and without sounding big-headed, I've been told I have a lot of work to do in getting information out. It is my role to do exactly as I am doing now, teaching and explaining in my way.'

When I mentioned the book *Conversations with Caesar* in which the soul of Julius Caesar communicated his story from the afterlife, John was most enthusiastic about this form of information exchange. 'There's so many good books being put out now, and spirit are doing a lot of work here, making contact with people like yourself who are willing and able.'

I wondered about the reason for the increased contact between earth and the afterlife and John said that the earthly world needs a lot of help now, as it is in a bad way, and people are suffering. Fortunately, on earth we are in a great time of spiritual awareness. There is a wonderful opportunity now, and John said there are many souls like him helping to spread information about the afterlife. He described some of the different ways being employed to get the message across as talking, channelling and straight-forward guidance. He spoke enthusiastically about the process of placing thoughts in writers' heads. People in spirit are not concerned that a writer thinks *they* have come up with amazing information, and take all the credit. The importance is in the words.

When I enquired about the existence of any authorities or rule-makers, John said there is an organised form of behaviour, but it is more of an understanding of the way things need to be. When he first crossed over John was instructed in the ways of the afterlife by several souls from a much higher level than he was at that point. Since then he has advanced to a new level, because of the lessons he has learned. He quietly told me it is not something to brag about, as everyone is there to learn.

John described his current status a little enigmatically as being at a 'certain position in learning', and he thrives on it, emphasising that we as souls never stop learning.

'Learning is not seen as a horrendous, difficult thing . . . oh, God, we gotta go to school today. People almost run to class, they want to be the first there,' he explained. 'The life here is the fun. I'm not saying it's all wonderful. There are difficult times, there are mistakes made, same as in a human life. But I can go sailing or swimming or play tennis whenever I want. The life here *is* fun, it's real, it's inspirational.'

John agreed with my earlier description of the afterlife as being a giant learning resort, where nobody really wants to leave. He confirmed the living conditions are 'however you want them to be'. If he wanted to be where he lived on earth, right on the waterfront, in a waterfront house, fishing off the wharf, he could do it.

John loves going to what he described as 'an old-fashioned outdoor cinema' to watch films under a beautiful starlit sky. Most of the films he watches have an educational theme with a real meaning to them. 'I wouldn't say there's action films here,' he said with a chuckle. 'No shoot 'em up type movies; more down to earth themes. But if I want to go to my home and watch *Gone With the Wind,* so be it.' He said he has now lost his craving to watch any mainstream films, including his own productions. There are documentaries available, and he found these truly inspiring to watch.

When speaking about his 'normal' activities, he found it a little difficult to explain in terms we would understand. 'I'll put it this way,' he said. 'I spend a lot of time with other souls, or to put it another way, other *people*, talking, discussing, debating. I may be doing this for a certain amount of time. There is no such thing as time, no real night and day. I can't say I did that for a day, as there is no day. If you want a night time, need a night time, you can have a night time.'

John confirmed the concept of time, which is paramount in earthly life, is totally irrelevant in the afterlife and there is no time in the world of spirit. He believes that this very simple concept can be so difficult for people to understand, and added that he still divides time into night and day, because this is where he is in his progression, but everyone can create what they want.

During his past-life review John discovered his previous lives had been varied. The first life he saw was as a female, and then a child who never made it past childhood. He trailed off here, not wanting to pursue the details of the past, preferring instead to concentrate on the present. He said in the afterlife they teach the reasons behind our past actions. Some of his greatest learning has been focusing on his last life, 'The mistakes I made—and there were many—and the good I did. It's just a never-ending cycle here of learning, looking at past lives and indeed future lives.'

When asked whether he would be reincarnating, he said, 'Absolutely, I will be coming back. I don't get to know yet in what form.' He went on to say it is a lot easier not knowing right now, but there was a lot of preparation for one's next life, and he was a long way from that.

According to John the difficult part is going back into the human body and having another life. When we are in the world of spirit no one wants to leave, but that journey into the human body is part of our development, so it is considered a natural progression.

'When we understand this we can accept it,' he said. 'If we had a choice here everyone would say, "No, I'd love to stay here, this is the good time. Please don't make me go back to a body with the pain and the mistakes."'

He reflected for a moment before continuing: 'The physical pain like I had with the cancer, why would you want to go back and experience all that?'

45

Leaving loved ones behind

During his visit, John revealed to us that in the initial stages of passing over, the need to stay in touch with family and friends on earth can have an 'unbelievable pull'. So much so that some people will almost physically take themselves back to earth. He described these cases being like a ghost in a house or something similar, when someone so desperately wants to hang on to the life they had.

As souls in spirit progress, and the need to stay with loved ones still living fades, many like to visit earth only to keep an eye on things. People in the afterlife, John said, still feel the need to help their friends and family, not wanting them to make mistakes. It doesn't matter whether they left a partner who later remarries, the love is still there. People in spirit sometimes can see mistakes coming and want to help, so there is always a connection. However, they are not allowed to help without permission from higher spirits.

They have to explain the situation and it is then thought through. Intervention is only allowed if it is deemed in that person's highest possible good, otherwise permission will be refused.

John explained it is possible for a visiting soul to interfere and influence the outcome of some event in a human life, but this is not permitted, as it could create chaos: 'You just can't visit a loved one and follow them around the kitchen whispering "don't drive that car this morning" until they listen.' He told us that if a spirit did interfere in someone's life on earth without permission, they would be in a lot of trouble. 'Everyone has free will, even in the world of spirit, but we have to take responsibility for our actions.'

I asked John to confirm that certain events are known in advance to those in spirit. 'Yes, and I guess you would deem that as having psychic abilities,' he said with a chuckle, 'but that is one of the perks of being here.'

With all the activities in the afterlife how do they manage to stay in touch with us to know about forthcoming events? John answered in his usual direct way. 'You're allowed to look in on your family and friends, to give love, support and to have that communication. Whilst you're doing this, certain information will come to you which you can take to your teachers.' John says all souls have a certain psychic ability. Some have simply developed their psychic ability further than others.

John also told us that when people first pass over they are assigned a certain teacher, but these teachers change as they progress in their soul growth. So if someone knew an accident was about to happen, they could go to this teacher and ask for permission to help their loved one avoid it. However, the accident may be part of their loved one's karma, where the person needs to learn a lesson, or perhaps it is their time to pass over, in which case permission would not be given.

It's also possible to ask the teacher whether the person on earth can learn the lesson any other way. The teacher may then need to consult their own superiors, to discover whether this is indeed possible. 'Everyone has a superior, as in human life,' John added. 'It works its way up the chain.'

When asked about the role bureaucracy plays in the afterlife, John said, 'It's needed in a certain way, because everyone is at a certain level in their life.' Then he went on to say, 'Things are complex, but they are also simple. There is a structure, there is a format, and there are definitely rules. You cannot just come here and do whatever you like.'

Again the message is quite clear—as above, so below.

46

John's take on religion

When I asked John about the existence of religions in the afterlife and also whether he had ever seen or had contact with any of the great masters—Jesus, Buddha or Mohammed—his reply was very forthright. 'What you learn is that there is no such thing as any religion here.'

John said those people who have been highly religious in life discover the ideals or ideas of those particular religions rarely work. 'People don't need to be a part of those to function properly,' he said. 'On the contrary people can function a lot better by releasing their previous belief systems.'

He added, 'When you say all of humanity is as one, or every soul is as one, it basically means you are all striving for the same thing to want to help mankind, to want to help each other. You're all part of the same team, whereas what is taught on earth is that everyone is all on separate teams. They're all at each other, trying to see who is the best. How can that possibly be?'

As for encountering any of the Ascended Masters, John struggled to provide a simple answer to what he termed a complex question. He gains inspiration from a number of teachers from higher levels who come and go. People in spirit are taught it is possible to get to their purest state. John describes this progress for each soul as, 'a striving, a cleansing, to get to our most wonderful essence that Jesus and other Ascended Masters would represent'.

He said people with dogmatic beliefs can be some of the most difficult people to help in the afterlife and some of the slowest learners. In earth terms John said, 'They can be sitting around for years, still going to church, still feeling they need those institutions.' He explained that because of their closed minds, they cannot accept the afterlife for what it really is. However, even the most narrow-minded souls do eventually come around, after being given special guidance.

It doesn't matter whether we have rigid beliefs or we believe in nothing, our state of mind about the afterlife will determine our initial entry point. So, what happens to this kind of church leader when they pass over?

John said most of them go to a special place in the afterlife, with teachers who are designed to do nothing more than talk and discuss. He described some of these religious leaders as very powerful people, who have been in places of influence at various times in history. Those who have abused their power will go to yet another area.

When asked about his knowledge of the lower astral plane, John explained that there are many different terms used to describe this level. 'There is a place some people go to, particularly people who have done some very, very bad things. They spend a long time there.' John, however, was quick to dismiss the notion of hell, adding that these souls are separated and not able to mix with others, but it is not punishment, they experience compassionate teaching, as they will need a lot more help than anyone else.

John was not prepared to reveal any names or details, saying that they are taught to avoid gossip in the afterlife. However, he did say that certain people who have just passed over, and are still attached to earthly life, will gossip all day long. But they do discover after a certain period in the spirit world that there is just no point to gossiping. It has absolutely no benefit and on the contrary is degrading and demeaning.

John had one final strong point to make about those people who cross over from a highly religious background thinking they are headed for heaven while all the others are hell bound. I could almost see the twinkle in his eyes as he said, 'They're in for a shock.'

47

Knowing when souls are crossing over

My final question to John was whether they know in the afterlife when we are about to leave the body and cross over.

'Again if we were talking time, you might have a couple of weeks before somebody passes,' he replied. 'There is a lot of discussion about how this person is going to handle their transition, and what your job is. I mean, even though I'm low on the pecking order I still help.'

John said that sometimes he is asked to act as a guide. Even the simplest knowledge he possesses can still be of help to people who pass over because he has at least had that particular experience. He is able to comfort newly arrived souls, and sometimes help them connect with family and friends.

He said if you are selected to help, you are given background knowledge on the situation at hand. So, does this confirm that our lives do have a kind of contract, an agreed time of departure from each lifetime?

John replied without hesitating. 'Absolutely. How else would we be given the information that somebody is going to pass. It happens every time . . . at the time we are told.'

However, as John recognised, sometimes there are unexpected events, apart from someone knowingly taking their own life. 'There are accidents, not everything is foreseen. People do veer off their path and do things completely unpredictably.'

These events can include complications like alcohol, drugs and even medication. John told us that in these cases there is often no warning or control in the afterlife. 'It's a very sad thing, because someone who is meant to perhaps live to an old age, and have all sorts of lessons in life, to help people and such, can have it cut terribly short.'

When they arrive in the afterlife, these souls, often in a confused state, are given extensive guidance and counselling because of their actions. Then they have to go back for another life and often start again, learning and experiencing those lessons they missed.

As John said, 'Nothing is set in concrete, even though there was originally a contract.'

I found the contact with John Dingwell in the world of spirit to be enlightening and inspiring. He confirmed many of my own findings about the afterlife, not the least of which is the unique journey of discovery that we all make in between each life.

Part F
Preparing for the Next Life

48

When the time is right

'I am certain that I have been here as I am now a thousand times before, and I hope to return a thousand times.'
JOHANN WOLFGANG VON GOETHE, WRITER, 1749–1842

There comes a stage in our between-life sojourn when we have to start preparing for our next step. For some this means advancing to higher levels in the afterlife if they have been considered worthy of elevation by the Elders. The higher spheres are only accessible if we gain this permission.

Most souls are quite content with staying in the comfort of the spheres closer to the earth where they can enjoy a peaceful, pleasant existence until it is time to reincarnate. But there are those more interested in moving onward and upward. They discover there are levels within levels to be accessed when a soul has earned a promotion.

Once we have advanced to certain levels, there is no need for us to reincarnate unless we choose to. Activities on these higher levels take us into caring roles such as guides, healers and teachers.

Highly qualified souls are also given permission to help out with development back on earth. Scientists are always working on new advances, which are developed before being passed on to their earthly counterparts, through thought-transference or the dream state. The same applies to medical breakthroughs, engineering developments, technical inventions and so on. Former doctors who are now in spirit work not only with those in the afterlife, but also assist in operations on earth. Other doctors in spirit may get approval to 'sit in' on operations in hospitals when invited, and also in personal and group healings. As one eminent doctor in spirit told me in a channelled session, 'You only have to ask'.

A friend of mine was told by this same doctor in Brazil that he would attend the delicate operation of his six-year-old son back in Australia and that there was nothing to worry about. During the subsequent operation, which went far smoother than the attending doctors anticipated, a nurse was heard to say she thought the surgeon's hands were being guided. Not the kind of comment you would necessarily expect in an operating theatre.

For the vast majority of us the next stage of our soul journey means returning to earth. As wonderful as life is in the world of spirit, the average soul progresses far quicker through new human experiences on earth. There are many ways we learn on earth. Handling our many emotions, including our hidden fears, provides ample opportunity for soul growth. Progress is much slower when we stay in the afterlife, especially for those in the lower spheres, so our guides and the Council of Elders advise us accordingly. While it is not always compulsory to reincarnate, the soul is informed that it is in their best interests to do so. Sometimes a little extra coaxing is needed for those who have bad memories of previous lives to encourage them to take on a new set of circumstances. However, there are still choices offered to us for the kind of life we wish to lead and the contract we are prepared to make. This choice will also embrace our requirements for balancing any outstanding karma.

Some highly advanced souls are given the opportunity to experience lifetimes in other worlds, but most souls return to earth as part of their natural life cycle. As each inhabited planet has its own afterlife spheres, the opportunity to move on to other worlds has to be earned.

In our soul group meetings the time will eventually arrive when our guide takes us aside and informs us we are now ready for the next earthly adventure. For some it might be preceded by a whisper in our consciousness, or simply a feeling that 'it is time to go back'. At this point some souls protest and ask for more time to prepare, while others are keen to embrace a new body and anticipate new adventures.

An important step is to meet with the Council of Elders again, who have been following your progress since you crossed over, much like the placement committee of a management consultancy. Having decided what you need to experience and learn, the Elders are the ones who confirm with you the nature of your next role in the ongoing theatre of life.

For many people this is a time of excitement and anticipation, although it can be a time of great challenge, as they are about to leave a world of peace, compassion and wonderful support for a life which offers hardships, overwhelming obstacles and complex situations. This, of course, can be tempered with the physical delights not available in the afterlife. Not everything on earth is hard going, especially if the soul retains keen memories of the fun side of life from past incarnations. For some it may also mean meeting up with old friends and family members who have already reincarnated.

To prepare for this we undertake a series of exercises with our guides and soul companions, like a kind of 'role playing'. By now we are familiar with our karmic situation, and so guidance is then given on how to respond to certain potential events and situations in our next life.

We agree to play various roles in each others' lives, so we can all learn and grow as spiritual beings. This may mean that someone you think is your adversary or being unfair to you on earth could actually be a dear soul friend who is doing you a big favour by providing opportunities for growth. I remember reading a channelled angelic message which had a big impact on me that simply stated, 'Human beings have chosen to learn and grow through adversity.'

All this preparation is not retained by the conscious mind once we eventually embrace a new body, as it would be too overwhelming. However, the higher self retains all this information and, once we meet the situations and challenges previously agreed on, we have the opportunity to respond in a much more favourable manner. This inter-life training encourages us to look for answers before rushing blindly into a situation, to listen instead to the still, small voice within.

There is no set duration for each sojourn in the afterlife for us to rest, recuperate, review and prepare for the next adventure. What we do know is that we spent much longer periods between lives in ancient times. Of course, the earth's population was much thinner then.

Now with nearly seven billion people on the planet, souls are being 'recycled' a lot quicker. In my own case the time spent in the afterlife following my last incarnation was only 26 earth years. Regression stories tell of people presently on the planet who died during World War II. Some have huge karmic debts to balance.

Word from the afterlife is that we need never worry about running out of souls. Earth is only one of many inhabited planets in the cosmos, despite what we are led to believe by certain so-called authorities. The universe also teems with many types of life. As earth is becoming more advanced it has also become more attractive to souls from other worlds who wish to experience life in this domain.

As for souls returning as animals or even insects, I've been told this simply does not happen. Animals reincarnate as animals and once you have evolved into a human soul you cannot go backwards.

Speaking of animals, yes, our pets do have a special dimension in the afterlife and there are many happy reports of owners being overjoyed when they are reunited with their departed animal friends. Animals may also be reincarnated to rejoin their favourite humans on earth.

Animal communicator Trisha McCaugh told me that my cat Apollo was the reincarnation of my previous cat Alex, who was tragically run over at a young age. We were so close that he apparently wanted to come back and complete our time together. Trisha told me this is not an uncommon event.

Sadly Apollo suffered the same fate. A lovely postscript to his death happened as I was bringing his body home from the vet's surgery where he passed away. As I rounded a corner near home a large handwritten sign was attached to a tree. In bold writing it proclaimed, 'Welcome Home Alex'.

As Trisha reminded me later, the universe has many ways of sending us messages.

As we have discovered, each journey into the afterlife, as well as the experiences in between incarnations, is unique. This may sound like a 'cop out' but when you consider our life on earth, it is exactly the same story. We may be collectively as one in our soul essence, but we each experience life in all its complexity as an individual adventure.

In a lovely unplanned meditation shortly before finishing this book, I looked back on my current life, mainly from the time I left school and started working. At the end of this experience, some 60 minutes later, I realised my marvellous life has been like a gigantic rolling wave, taking me from one major situation to the next in a continual, flowing motion. I thanked my guide for this experience as I have much to be grateful for in this lifetime. It is a life completely different to my previous existence as Brian. A life I have created from my free will and one where I am happy to take complete responsibility for its outcome.

49

On the road again

So, what of Brian? Markus arrived at Brian's villa to inform him that the Elders had decided he was to return to earth for his next life fairly soon, and that he would shortly meet with the Council again to be given more details. In the meantime, the Elders wanted Brian to concentrate on his life lessons and not concern himself with too much extra work.

At the time he was helping former soldiers in the healing centres, who had passed over from wounds suffered in the Great War. As some of these men had lingered in service hospitals for several years after the war ended before eventually passing over, they were still in a bad way. Brian had mixed feelings about giving up this work, as these troubled souls always appreciated being with other former soldiers, and he was able to help them in their adjustment to their new conditions. However, orders are orders.

This time Brian and Markus did not have to go to the Elders. Two came to Brian, instead. He was sitting in a darkened space in the Hall of Records, when suddenly he felt their presence beside him. In a sense he could also see them—this time they looked more like glowing lights. He got the distinct impression that they wanted this session to be more intimate, so that he was relaxed and did not feel like he was being summoned before the Council. Mr Gladstone was the main spokesman. He was joined by a loving female elder, referred to by Mr Gladstone as 'Mercy'.

They told Brian there was another war coming on earth and felt it would be appropriate for him to be born in the middle of it this time. They showed Brian two alternatives. The first was a life in a fairly wild and remote part of northern India. It would be another short life, but this time he could be a kind of monk and spend his days in spiritual and mystical pursuits. He could advance very quickly during this life, but it would not be easy.

The second choice was a much longer lifespan in the southern hemisphere, where he would be given the opportunity of having many experiences. His life would have two parts, with the second half aimed more at spiritual development and helping others. The only thing Brian associated with Australia was a picture of a kangaroo he had once seen in a book. He had also met a few Aussies in the trenches and they were a cheerful bunch.

The Elders told Brian that both lives would give him the opportunity to look within and learn a lot about himself. For Brian it was easy, and with no hesitation he chose to live in Australia. After making his decision the Elders told Brian that Markus would give him special lessons in preparation for this life. He would also receive their blessing and guidance and have the opportunity to resolve some karma from past relationships. In fact, an important theme in his next life would be in handling many different kinds of relationships.

The session concluded with Brian being shown glimpses of several relationships with people that he would encounter from past lifetimes. He was particularly pleased to hear he had gained a lot of experience and wisdom from these lives that would help him with this next incarnation. This knowledge would be integrated into his final training sessions for the life awaiting him.

As I contemplated what lay ahead, I was under no illusions that my life as the young soldier Brian was like a grain of sand on the beach.

50
Unanswered questions

At this stage of my research, I still had several unan-swered questions about my inter-life journey and the souls I met there. I asked my guide M to help me resolve them. M took me first to the little Greek village where Brian was preparing for his next incarnation. It was a very strange experience watching another aspect of 'myself'. It was as if I was watching a stage play, but also involved with it as well. Brian's mother had been released from the healing centre and was staying with him. The gulf between Brian and his two brothers remained from his last life; they lived on a different level in spirit.

While life was hardly all work and no play, the emphasis for Brian was definitely on preparing for what was to come. His soul family were all part of this preparation. I recognised the astral energy of my son Matt (in my current life) return to join in with these preparations from time to time, even though he himself had incarnated back on earth recently. Brian had been told earlier Matt's earthly life was to be a short life and that he would be back in spirit just before I was to be born. He agreed to be my son in this upcoming life and we would be an ongoing part of each other's lives.

I also briefly encountered the soul energy of the person who was to be my daughter in this life. She was nearing the end of a long life on earth at the time and visited Brian's soul family while she was in the dream state.

Another soul also joined the group and I instantly recognised my brother Michael from my current life. While not in my direct soul family, his soul group has close links with mine, and we had been together in several past lives. I saw how we are two very different soul types, which has played out in our current lives. Michael has been an explorer and adventurer in the past and needs to break new ground in his soul's journey. Yet, in spite of the differences, there is a great closeness between us now. It turned out we had been brothers, even brothers-in-arms, in several past lives.

As the group worked together it became evident to me watching from the sidelines that life is like a giant jigsaw puzzle. M actually showed me a complex picture of life being similar to a giant tapestry, with many threads being woven together as events unfold. He emphasised the importance of staying with the central part of the tapestry and not trying to get too far ahead of yourself in life, as you will only get confused. In other words, we need to let life evolve by staying focused on the present. People get stressed about so much in life, often unnecessarily. By relaxing and letting things unfold, the big picture will emerge when the time is right.

This particularly applies to love relationships. I have done readings for so many people who are impatient to meet the partner of their dreams. I do my best to assure them that when the time is right they will meet the right partner, as more than likely they have arranged it before they were even born. Souls agree on meeting times and places to get together, and even have pre-arranged signals such as a touch, a glance, a subconscious memory or one of a thousand other subliminal signs.

When I met Judy neither of us took much notice of the other one for the first couple of weeks, despite the manipulations of her friend who had introduced us. Then, at a birthday dinner for her friend, we both looked at each other simultaneously and something just clicked. Judy confided later that she knew then she would spend the rest of her life with me. This proved to be true.

I asked M about Judy as we observed Brian's soul group at work. I presumed that she was a member of my soul family, but had not recognised her energy in the group at that stage. He seemed bemused and informed me that

Judy was my mother. A little slow on the uptake I queried how that could possibly be the case as Judy was with me when my mother passed over. He looked at me the way you would at a child asking a naïve question. 'Not your current life. The soul energy that is Judy was your mother in your last life and was the one you visited in hospital.'

I was stunned, as I had come to believe that our soul mates are very rarely reincarnated as our parents. M agreed this was normally not the case, but said it does sometimes happen. This helped explain why Brian's mother passed over so quickly when he was killed in the war. We do not always immediately recognise souls the way we remember them, but there is always a spiritual recognition factor. I can only assume that I slipped up there because of the vast amount of information I was being shown. Mind you it still leaves me with a strange feeling to come to terms with.

One person that suddenly went missing from my group was the lovely Fleur, but M told me that she, too, had reincarnated for a brief lifetime. Apparently this does happen occasionally. Souls just disappear for a while without any fuss. I asked M at what stage of history the earth was experiencing and he said it was the early 1930s. He told me Fleur would only be on earth for about three years and would return before I was to reincarnate. As she was to play only a small but important part in my next life, we did not need to do a lot of preparation.

The soul energy of Brian was 'introduced' to the couple who would be his parents in the next life. As we watched from the sidelines, M told me that once a woman becomes pregnant the combined parental energy is beamed to the spirit world where it is received and catalogued by what he termed 'the record keepers'. Once a life choice is made each soul is normally placed with appropriate parents which, of course, determines the environment and conditions under which they will be born into and embrace.

Brian had already been shown visions of potential directions and destiny points to help in his decision for this next life, but M explained that whatever choice he had made, the main purpose of this life was to be around teaching, learning and helping others by utilising various forms of communications.

I watched as Brian met with his future parents in their astral form, as, of course, they were already on earth. Then Brian started preparing for his rebirth in earnest.

51
The next life

After this all too brief sojourn in the world of spirit it was time to make final preparations for Brian's return to earth. Anticipating a final briefing session with the Council of Elders, Brian was rather surprised to find himself in the presence of only one member. It is always difficult to tell the gender of these wonderful beings, but he was sensing the very feminine energy of Mercy.

His next life would be lived mainly in a big coastal city, where there was lots of sunshine and beaches. Brian was drawn to the soul energy of the person who would be his mother. She was only young and was about to farewell her husband off to war. There was an immediate empathy towards her. As the thought of war came to mind, Brian was relieved that he would grow up in a post-war atmosphere, with no possibility of being involved in further conflict.

During pregnancy the spirit normally comes and goes from the foetus, until the time of birth. This helps the bond between mother and child, and prevents the spirit from getting bored just hanging around waiting. It is also the final opportunity for last minute training and direct interaction with our soul family. The exact time the soul finally locks in to place seems to vary. Some people who were being regressed at the time report that they only 'clocked in' as the birth was taking place.

When Brian learned that both his mother and Fleur were also reincarnating to the same city during this period, he was very pleased. Even though they would only have fairly brief times together, it was enough. Mercy was very satisfied with Brian's progress in spirit and told Markus to start the wheels turning for Brian's return.

This involved some direct familiarisation with his new parents but he was only able to spend a little time with them during their dream state. The connection with his future mother was very strong, but he did not really relate very well with his father-to-be. He was a very quiet, almost distant man who had grown up in 'a broken home'. Long before arriving on earth again, Brian knew getting to know his future father would be a challenge, but he also knew that at heart his father was a very decent and honourable person, and would always be supportive.

Brian was informed of the exact time and place of birth, which is an integral part of the planning process. We are all born at the precise moment decided on by the Elders, as they know best the importance of timing—something we're now aware of through such sciences as astrology and numerology.

Then, at last, time to go.

After he said his goodbyes to his soul family, Markus took Brian into a very private space and told him to lie down, let go of his thoughts and relax. He asked Markus if he would still be his guide during this next lifetime. Markus simply smiled and shook his head. He told Brian he would have new guides allocated to him. Brian felt a little sad, but was grateful for all that Markus had done for him and so they said their farewells.

Then the birth process began as Brian left the afterlife for his next adventure on earth.

52
One more time

As part of my research, Valerie, a past-life regression therapist, took me back to relive the whole birth experience. It was a very bizarre sensation as I was able to experience the process as if it were actually happening. What follows is what I went through in that session.

Alone in cocoon-like surroundings I soon drifted into what can only be described as a deep meditative state surrounded by a comforting blackness. The blackness eventually started to change colour, turning into a lovely kind of pink mist. I felt supported and very much loved as I drifted happily, and all thoughts of the past gradually faded away.

When asked to describe the conditions in the womb just before my birth, I saw the image of an eye watching and protecting me. By now I was surrounded by a soft shade of dark blue. My guide M later told me this eye was actually a representation of my higher self, that portion of my soul energy that was staying in spirit. He further confirmed that I had elected to bring about 75 to 80 per cent of my soul essence back to earth, the remainder stayed with my soul family as my higher self.

Now joined to the foetus, I was experiencing a feeling of restriction and was asked whether I was able to move. I confirmed I could move, but it wasn't easy. I tried to wriggle about to get comfortable. There was almost a sense of claustrophobia. 'I have been in here long enough, it is time to go,' I thought to myself. 'Just get on with it.'

My mother's womb was warm and it felt to me like I was an egg, a boiled egg. 'I want to breathe, to stretch, to see the sun.'

My eye tells me that everything is going to be OK. My eye stays with me, talking to me.

I feel even more restricted than before. The space is very tight. Then, after a pause, the sensation is of being sucked out of my mother, head first. I'm in a kind of tunnel. I've been here before. It's just like the tunnel to go home, same kind of tunnel. I can feel something there, drawing me, drawing me. I'm ready, but it's pretty tight. My shoulders are stuck. They're pulling on my head, which is not very good. Ooh, it's very bright out there.

By now I'm sort of halfway out of my mother. Somebody just said, 'He's very big.' My shoulders are out, but my hips are stuck now. There's this wiggling process going on . . . and now I'm out. I pause and there's big intake of breath. 'Ooh, I'm breathing. Ooh.'

After a few moments the realisation came to me. 'I'm back again. I'm back, back down here again. There's a pain in my head, where they pulled me out, behind my right ear.'

A feeling of happiness then embraced me. 'It's good to be back, I'm glad I decided to come back. I've got a lot to do, but in this life I have plenty of time to do it. One more time.'

Afterword

For most of my life I have been aware of a subconscious call to visit the World War I battlefields in France. After writing *Afterlife* I decided it was time to make that journey.

There were still ghosts of the past that needed to be put to rest and I was determined to see where Brian had perished on that fateful day in 1916. It was as if the spirit energies that guided and assisted my writing had decided there were still lessons to be learned.

Holidaying in England with my partner the week prior to our visit I was recommended *Birdsong* by Sebastian Faulks. An epic tale of bravery and endurance it was set in the Somme, you guessed it, in 1916 in the lead-up to the bloody battles in which Brian and his mates fought and died. The graphic descriptions of life in the trenches synchronised with my own experiences and memories—a perfect precursor to visiting the Somme.

In another piece of synchronicity, Peter Smith, the guide who took us around the Somme historic sites, turned out to be an expert on the Devonshire regiments in which Brian was a soldier.

Peter met us at Albert railway station on a beautiful, sunny day. We climbed into his 4WD and drove towards the battlefields. In a meditation the previous night I had asked M to be with us and help me discover what I needed to know at this stage of my life. As we drove through the towns and villages, Peter was amazed that we had most sites to ourselves, despite it being the August holiday season. It was as if the way had been cleared for me to have a quiet, intimate spiritual experience.

Approaching the Devonshire Cemetery in Mametz was very emotional for me. Gazing out over the adjoining wide, open and exposed fields where the infamous battle had been fought brought a lump to my throat. How could anyone possibly survive an attack in these circumstances? The generals who had organised those attacks must have known they were sending countless men into a maelstrom of death. It made me angry to think of such callous decisions being made, resulting in such disaster.

We walked slowly and silently along a pathway leading us up a small hill to the Devonshire cemetery, where we were finally able to reflect on those fateful words: 'The Devonshires held this trench. The Devonshires hold it still.'

After that torturous battle the Devons buried their dead near where they had fallen. The site was the forward trench, where the attack had begun. They erected a wooden cross and added their special inscription. Those words have since been solidified into sandstone, at the secluded entrance to the cemetery, within a protective grove of trees, where I now stood with a wildly beating heart.

After telling Peter I wanted some time alone to 'reconnect with an old ancestor' I slowly walked along the rows of gravestones looking at the names of the fallen.

At the far end of the cemetery was a mass grave where many unidentified bodies had been laid to rest after the battle. As I stood looking at this grassed plot a huge wave of emotion swept over me and the tears starting pouring down my cheeks. M came into my thoughts and confirmed this was indeed the place where Brian's remains were buried, along with his mates.

After spending some quiet time in contemplation, I was able to compose myself enough to look at the other graves. Pausing in front of the headstone of Lieutenant William Hodgson, a young man not much older than Brian, I read the poem he had written just before the attack. It was a heartfelt plea to God to help him die like a man and my emotions were stirred yet again.

As I wandered quietly through the cemetery the saddest aspect was to see the number of soldiers between 18 and 22 who were slain in that battle. Young men cut down before they had a chance to live life, not given the chance to develop their latent talents. Who is to say that William Hodgson may have turned out to be a brilliant writer had he lived? The only skill all had developed was to kill and maim.

While standing there for some time, I experienced a range of turbulent emotions. To my amazement, I then began to come to terms with what had happened in those dark times, and started to feel a lot lighter in spirit. I felt as if I was emerging from a murky, gloomy and misty environment.

So much of my life I'd felt as if I'd been driving forward with one eye constantly on the rear vision mirror. I had been consistently aware of great agitation with things creeping up on me and unexpectedly erupting, like bombshells. When I eventually walked slowly away from the cemetery I did not look back, and knew I had much to look forward to.

Thinking back on this memorable visit I can now say without hesitation that I have cleared a blockage that has been there all my life. I am now able to finally move on from my past and my fascination with World War I and all its horrors.

Finally in the Somme in 2010, I have been able to stand in the shadow of a large sandstone cross, within the well-maintained memorial of the Devonshire cemetery and view its trimmed lawns and commemorative headstones. I was able to ease the heartache and appreciate the beautiful red roses there, nodding in the gentle breeze.

Notes

Preface

1. See <www.noetic.org> for more details.
2. My internet radio program *RadioOutThere.com* covers all aspects of mind, body and spirit and has been on air in both mainstream radio and the internet since 1997.

Chapter 4: The soul's path

1. Carolyn Evers, *Conversations with Caesar*, Cosmic Connections, 2004, pp. 3–5.

Chapter 6: Where do we go after death?

1. Seth is a spirit channelled by Jane Roberts in a series of books over several decades: Jane Roberts, *Seth Speaks: The eternal validity of the soul*, Prentice-Hall, 1972.

Chapter 7: The vastness of the spirit world

1. See <www.johnofgod.com> for more details.
2. The Monroe Institute is a non-profit education and research organisation devoted to the exploration of human consciousness, based in Faber, Virginia. See <www.monroeinstitute.org> for more details.

Chapter 8: Where we fit in

1. Ian Lawton, *The Wisdom of the Soul*, Rational
    Spirituality, 2007, pp. 58–60.

Chapter 9: Is suicide punished?

1. Deepak Chopra, *Life After Death: The burden of proof*,
    Random House, 2006.
2. T. Lobsang Rampa, *I Believe*, Corgi Books, 1976, pp.
    34–41.

Chapter 13: The tunnel linking both worlds

1. Diane Goble, *Through the Tunnel: A traveler's guide
    to spiritual rebirth*, S.O.U.L. Foundation, Inc., 1993.
    See <www.beyondtheveil.net> for more details.
2. Trypheyna McShane, co-author of *The Intimacy of Death
    and Dying*, Allen & Unwin, 2009.

Chapter 18: Inside the healing centre

1. Jane Roberts, *Seth Speaks*, Amber-Allen, 1994, p. 129.

Chapter 20: God and the afterlife

1. Robert A. Monroe, *Journeys Out of the Body*, Doubleday,
    1971. Robert A. Monroe is the founder of the Monroe
    Institute.
2. F. Holmes Atwater, *Captain of My Ship, Master of My
    Soul: Living with guidance*, Hampton Roads, 2001.
3. Robert Monroe, *Journeys Out of the Body*.

Chapter 25: Meeting the Council of Elders

1. In what might be regarded as synchronicity, several
    months after hearing about Mr Gladstone I watched
    the film *Khartoum*, the story of General Gordon, on
    DVD. In the film Gordon was sent to relieve the siege

of Khartoum in 1884, by the British prime minister, William Gladstone. An interesting side note is that General Gordon believed in reincarnation. In 1877, he wrote in a letter: 'This life is only one of a series of lives which our incarnated part has lived. I have little doubt of our having pre-existed; and that also in the time of our pre-existence we were actively employed. So, therefore, I believe in our active employment in a future life, and I like the thought.'

2.   Bob Olson is the editor of *OfSpirit.com*.

Chapter 26: Soul families and soul mates

1.   Several months after writing this chapter I read Bruce Moen's book *Voyages into the Afterlife* (Hampton Roads, 1999), where he recounts his experience of the same situation on Focus 27 with his guide White Bear.

2.   Michael Newton, *Journey of Souls: Case studies of life between lives*, Llewellyn, 1994, pp. 87–90.

Chapter 30: Unlimited opportunities

1.   Sylvia Browne, *Conversations with the Other Side*, Hay House, 2002, pp. 63–4.

Chapter 31: Fun and entertainment

1.   See <www.cfpf.org.uk>.

2.   Victor Zammit, *A Lawyer Presents the Case for the Afterlife: Irrefutable objective evidence*, Gammell, 2002.

3.   Bruce Moen in an interview with the author on *RadioOutThere.com*, 18 June 2009.

Chapter 32: Is there sex over there?

1.   Sylvia Browne, *Life on the Other Side*, Penguin, 2002, pp. 134–5.

Chapter 33: Religion and the afterlife

1. Victor Zammit, *A Lawyer Presents the Case for the Afterlife*.

Chapter 34: Just another day in paradise

1. Robert Murray, *The Stars Still Shine: An afterlife journey*, Aura, 2000.
2. Published in Robert Murray's e-magazine *TheStarsStillShine.com* and reproduced in full with the permission of the author and publisher.

Chapter 35: A fisherman's story

1. A trance medium is able to leave the body and channel other beings or travel to the astral realms without being consciously aware at the time.

Chapter 36: Furthering our knowledge

1. Peter Ramster, *The Search for Lives Past*, Somerset Films and Publishing, 1990.

Chapter 39: Spirit healers

1. For more information on spirit doctors and helpers visit <www.johnofgod.com>.

Further reading

Sylvia Browne, *Conversations with the Other Side*, Hay House, 2002

Sylvia Browne, *Life on the Other Side*, Penguin, 2002

Ezio De Angelis, *Living Spirit*, 2007

Carolyn Evers, *Conversations with Caesar*, Cosmic Connections, 2004

Diane Goble, *Through the Tunnel: A traveler's guide to spiritual rebirth*, S.O.U.L. Foundation, Inc., 1993

F. Holmes Atwater, *Captain of My Ship, Master of My Soul: Living with guidance*, Hampton Roads, 2001

Ian Lawton, *The Book of the Soul*, Rational Spirituality, 2004

Ian Lawton, *The Wisdom of the Soul*, Rational Spirituality, 2007

Bruce Moen, *Voyages into the Afterlife*, Hampton Roads, 1999

Robert A. Monroe, *Journeys Out of the Body*, Doubleday, 1971

Robert Murray, *The Stars Still Shine: An afterlife journey*, Aura, 2000

Michael Newton, *Journey of Souls: Case studies of life between lives*, Llewellyn, 1994

Michael Newton, *Destiny of Souls: New case studies of life between lives*, Llewellyn, 2000

Peter Ramster, *The Search for Lives Past*, Somerset Films and Publishing, 1990

Peter Ramster, *In Search of Lives Past*, Somerset Films and Publishing, 1992

Neville Randall, *Life After Death*, Robert Hale & Co., 2001

Jane Roberts, *Seth Speaks: The eternal validity of the soul*, Prentice-Hall, 1972

Neale Donald Walshe, *Conversations With God*, Hachette, 1999

Gary Williams, *Life Beyond Death*, Robert Hale & Co., 1989

Victor Zammit, *A Lawyer Presents the Case for the Afterlife: Irrefutable objective evidence*, Gammell, 2002

About the author

Barry Eaton has wide experience in all areas of the media and entertainment industries. He is a well-known radio and TV presenter, having spent many years with the ABC and various commercial radio and TV stations. His profile embraces news and sports anchoring, lifestyle shows, current affairs, talkback radio, as well as music and entertainment.

Currently he produces and presents a weekly internet radio program, *RadioOutThere.com*, embracing the metaphysical and the paranormal.

Former coordinator of the Faculty of Journalism at Macleay College in Sydney, Barry lectured in radio journalism and production from 1995 to 1999. He has also had wide corporate experience, running his own company, which incorporated media consultancy, video production, and special event marketing and publicity.

As a writer Barry has scripted and narrated many documentary films and corporate presentations. He specialises in lifestyle and other related features and has been published in many leading newspapers and magazines. His media consultancy experience included work with the Canadian government, Lauda air, the Tahiti Tourist Bureau, EMI, Environmental Solutions International, and Bleakleys (financial advisors).

He is in demand as a voice-over artist/actor and has narrated a series of wildlife documentaries which are often seen on cable TV. Visitors to the Australian War Memorial in Canberra will hear him narrating the video presentations in the new Korea and Vietnam gallery. Barry's voice is also heard guiding motorists on a GPS navigation system.

In 2006 he co-hosted the spectacular ANZAC Military Tattoo at Sydney's Acer Arena and then the Tattoo Spectacular in Perth in 2007. Barry originally trained as an actor and has appeared on stage and in several TV series and films.

Wearing his metaphysical hat, Barry is also a qualified astrologer and intuitive reader and conducted a meditation and development group in Sydney for ten years.